Accessing the General Curriculum

Second Edition

Accessing the General Curriculum

Second Edition

Including Students With Disabilities in Standards-Based Reform

Victor Nolet
Margaret J. McLaughlin

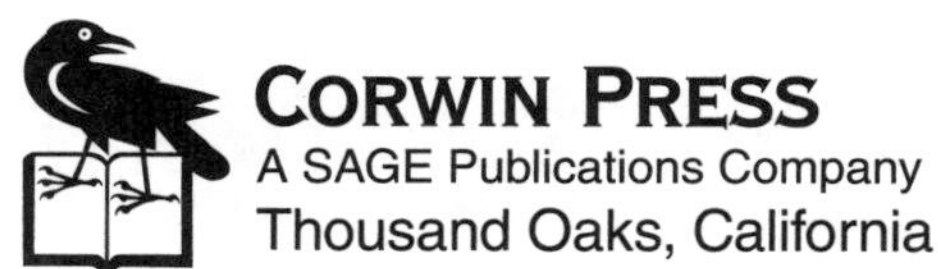

For information:

Corwin Press
A Sage Publications Company
2455 Teller Road
Thousand Oaks, California 91320
www.corwinpress.com

Sage Publications Ltd.
1 Oliver's Yard
55 City Road
London EC1Y 1SP
United Kingdom

Sage Publications India Pvt. Ltd.
B-42, Panchsheel Enclave
Post Box 4109
New Delhi 110 017 India

Printed in the United States of America

Library of Congress Cataloging-in-Publication Data

Nolet, Victor.
Accessing the general curriculum : including students with disabilities
in standards-based reform / Victor Nolet, Margaret J. McLaughlin.— 2nd ed.
p. cm.
Includes bibliographical references and index.
ISBN 978-1-4129-1648-6 (cloth)—ISBN 978-1-4129-1649-3 (pbk.)
1. Special education—Curricula—United States. 2. Children with disabilitieses—Education—United States. 3. Inclusive education—United States. I. Title.
LC3981.N65 2005
371.9′046—dc22

2005002288

This book is printed on acid-free paper.

10 9 8 7 6 5 4

Acquisitions Editor:	Robert D. Clouse
Editorial Assistant:	Jingle Vea
Production Editor:	Denise Santoyo
Copy Editor:	Colleen Brennan
Typesetter:	C&M Digitals (P) Ltd.
Indexer:	Pamela Van Huss
Cover Designer:	Anthony Paular

Contents

Acknowledgments

The authors would like to gratefully acknowledge the support and encouragement that we have received over the years from Robb Clouse at Corwin Press. It is Robb's unflagging confidence in our ideas and his unerring good judgment about how to present them that has made this book a reality.

Corwin Press appreciates the contributions of the following people:

Rosa Lockwood
Program Consultant
Ohio Office of Exceptional Children
Columbus, OH

Nora Bauer
Varying Exceptionalities Teacher
DeSoto Trail Elementary School
Tallahassee, FL

John Enloe
Director of Special Education
Sevier County School District
Sevierville, TN

Jane Adair
Resource Specialist
Long Beach Unified School District
Long Beach, CA

Judy Woodard
Special Education Teacher
Anderson Five School District
Anderson, SC

Mariella Brenlla
ESE Program Specialist
Miami Dade County Public Schools
Miami, FL

Paula Swanson
K-3 LAB Teacher
Patrick Henry School
Alexandria, VA

Art Arnold
Alaska State Special Education Director
Alaska Department of Education & Early Development
Juneau, AK

Lynne Everett
Consulting Teacher
Harding Avenue Elementary School
Blacksburg, VA

Kathy Bradberry
SPED Teacher
Darlington County School District
Darlington, SC

About the Authors

Victor W. Nolet is Director of Assessment and Evaluation for the Woodring College of Education at Western Washington University. He received his PhD from the University of Oregon. He has been a special educator for over 30 years. He began his career on a project to help individuals with mental retardation move from a state institution in Columbus, Ohio, into community settings. He has worked as a community-based mental retardation case worker and as a program coordinator in adult residential facilities. He has also worked extensively in public school settings, as a speech-language therapist, a high school resource room teacher, and as director of a regional program for high school students with intensive service needs. Nolet was on the faculty of the Department of Special Education at the University of Maryland for three years prior to joining the faculty at Western Washington University. His current interests focus on the impact of teacher education programs on preK–12 student outcomes and the impact of accountability systems on students with disabilities. He is currently investigating the characteristics of indicator systems that link the pre-service preparation of teachers to learning outcomes for public school students. He also is currently involved in an analysis of the validity of teacher work samples as measures of classroom-based practice for science and mathematics teachers. Nolet has served as Senior Consultant for the Educational Policy Reform Research Institute and has written and presented extensively on topics related to classroom-based assessment, assessment systems, and access to the general curriculum. In his spare time, Nolet plays old time and contra dance music on the fiddle, mandolin, and stand-up bass.

Margaret J. McLaughlin is Professor of Special Education and Associate Director, Institute for the Study of Exceptional Children and Youth, at the University of Maryland, College Park. She has been involved in special education all of her professional career, beginning as a teacher of students with serious emotional and behavior disorders. She earned her PhD at the University of Virginia and has held positions at the U.S. Office of Education and the University of Washington. She currently directs several national projects investigating educational reform and students with disabilities.

These include the national Educational Policy Reform Research Institute (EPRRI), a consortium involving the University of Maryland, The National Center on Educational Outcomes (NCEO), and the Urban Special Education Collaborative. EPRRI is studying the impact of high stakes accountability on students with disabilities. She is also directing a national research project investigating special education in charter schools and a Policy Leadership Doctoral and Postdoctoral Program in conducting large-scale research in special education. She has also worked in Bosnia, Nicaragua, and Guatemala in developing programs for students with developmental disabilities.

McLaughlin has consulted with numerous state departments of education and local education agencies on issues related to students with disabilities and the impact of standards-driven reform policies. She has cochaired the National Academy of Sciences (NAS) Committee on Goals 2000 and Students With Disabilities, which resulted in the report *Educating One and All.* She was a member of the NAS committee on the disproportionate representation of minority students in special education. She teaches graduate courses in disability policy and has written extensively in the area of school reform and students with disabilities.

Introduction

In 1997 and again in 2004 changes were made to the Individuals with Disabilities Education Act (IDEA) that were designed to strengthen the right of students who have disabilities to a free appropriate public education and to ensure greater accountability for those students. The law includes language that clearly communicates the expectation that special education must be connected to the general education curriculum. In fact, IDEA asserts that the education of students who have disabilities can be made more effective when schools ensure their access in the general curriculum to the maximum extent possible. The law also requires that students with disabilities participate in state and local assessments, with appropriate accommodations, or in an alternate assessment if necessary.

The IDEA clearly anchors special education in the general education curriculum and assessments and accountability. American schools are rapidly moving toward a system based on challenging standards, assessments, and high-stakes accountability for every student. Within this context, understanding what it means to provide "access" to the general education curriculum is more important that ever. If schools and individual students are held to higher expectations, then teachers must know how to provide every learner an opportunity to meet these new expectations.

1 Access to the General Education Curriculum

Why It Is More Important Than Ever Before

The purpose of this book is to help teachers and school administrators begin to translate policy into practice as we explore the meaning and implications of "access to the general education curriculum" and of ensuring that every student has an opportunity to access that curriculum. In this chapter, we are going to discuss the context for what it means to "access the general education curriculum." We are going to discuss the current legal and policy foundations and provide the important links between what teachers need to know and do in classrooms and the broader policy background. We will begin with the Individuals with Disabilities Education Act (IDEA) and then discuss the requirements of the new accountability reforms of the No Child Left Behind Act (NCLB).

IDEA AND ACCESS TO THE GENERAL EDUCATION CURRICULUM

IDEA has, in recent years, contained a number of new provisions that represent major advancements in ensuring that each student with a disability receives a high quality and individually designed education. The provisions build on the original purposes of law: Each student must be ensured a free appropriate public education; each child's education must be determined on an individualized basis and designed to meet his or her particular needs in the least restrictive environment; and the rights of children and their families must be ensured and protected through procedural safeguards. But, several changes have been made to better ensure that students with disabilities have access to a challenging curriculum and that their educational programs are based on high expectations. The Individuals with Disabilities Education Improvement Act of 2004

(IDEA) increased the focus of special education from simply ensuring access to education to improving the educational performance of students with disabilities and aligning special education services with the larger national school improvement efforts that include standards, assessments, and accountability.

New Individualized Education Program (IEP) Provisions. The Individualized Education Program (IEP) is the cornerstone of special education for any child and is critical to the success of a child's educational program. In 1997, and again in 2004, changes were made to the IEP provisions in IDEA that require specific attention to providing an individual student with a disability access to the general education curriculum. This requirement exists regardless of the setting in which the student will receive special education and related services.

Following is a synopsis of what an IEP must include:

- A statement of the child's present levels of academic achievement and functional performance, including how the disability affects the child's involvement and progress in the general education curriculum. (For preschool children, a statement of how the disability affects the child's participation in appropriate activities.) For children who take alternate assessments aligned to alternate achievement standards, a description of benchmarks or short-term objectives.
- Measurable annual goals, including academic and functional goals designed to enable the child to be involved in and progress in the general education curriculum; at the same time, they must meet all of the child's other unique educational needs.
- A statement of how the child's progress toward meeting the IEP annual goals will be measured and when periodic reports of the progress will be provided.
- A statement of the special education and related services, supplementary aids and services, based on peer-reviewed research to the extent possible, that are to be provided to the child. Also, a description of any modifications or supports for school personnel that are necessary for the child to advance toward attaining the annual goals, be involved and progress in the general education curriculum, participate in extracurricular or other nonacademic activities, and be educated and participate in activities with other children with and without disabilities.
- An explanation of the extent, if any, to which the child will not participate with the children without disabilities in general education classes and activities.
- A statement of any individual appropriate accommodations that are necessary to measure the academic achievement and functional performance of the child on state or district assessments. If the IEP team determines that the child shall take an alternate assessment, the IEP must include a statement that tells why the child cannot participate in the regular assessments and must indicate the alternate assessment that is selected.
- Appropriate measurable postsecondary goals beginning at age 16 or after.

IDEA and Participation in Assessments. IDEA requires that all children with disabilities be included in all state and district assessment programs with appropriate accommodations and alternate assessments where necessary as indicated in their IEPs. Specifically, states and local districts are required to include students with disabilities in the assessments required under Title I of the Elementary and Secondary Education Act of 2001 (The No Child Left Behind Act or NCLB). Both IDEA and Title I of NCLB provide specific requirements for how students with disabilities are to participate in assessments as well as how their scores are to be reported. Furthermore, IDEA and NCLB define alternate assessments as aligned with the state academic content standards and student achievement standards.

States and districts are required to report the performance of students with disabilities on state and district assessments, including alternate assessments, in the same detail that they use to report the performance of nondisabled students. Reporting and accountability requirements of NCLB apply equally to the subgroup of students with disabilities. IDEA clearly communicates that state and local assessments are to be regarded as educational benefits that contribute to a student's opportunity to learn challenging academic content. Moreover, IDEA supports NCLB in ensuring that schools are accountable for the achievement of students in special education and clearly signals the intent of federal policymakers to raise expectations for students with disabilities and improve their educational outcomes.

THE NO CHILD LEFT BEHIND ACT

The federal NCLB is the 2001 version of the Elementary and Secondary Education Act (ESEA), which was first passed in 1965. Title I of this law has always been concerned with creating educational equity for low-income children, and as the largest federal program in U.S. schools, it has had a major influence on the policies in K–12 education. In the early 1990s, a number of changes were made to Title I in an effort to promote greater equity between students in high poverty schools and other students. The changes were based on a vision of education referred to as standards-driven reform, which has been the dominant model for reform for almost two decades. In 2001, NCLB reinforced the vision of standards-driven reform and created even greater demands for states to create challenging standards and to require more accountability on the part of schools and school systems. To understand the requirements under NCLB, you will need to understand the components of standards-driven reform.

The Components of Standards-Driven Reform

Standards-driven reform has three critical components: (a) challenging content and achievement standards, (b) assessments aimed at measuring how schools are helping students meet the standards, and (c) accountability for achieving higher levels of student performance.

Standards. The defining element of standards-driven reform is the content and achievement standards. Standards are general statements of what students should know or be able to do as a result of their public school education. Content standards refer to what gets taught, the subject matter, the skills and knowledge, and the applications. They reflect the professional judgment of educators and the community at large about what really matters in education. Achievement standards set the targets or levels of performance that students must achieve in the content. Achievement standards set the targets for teaching. They specify that "by the time students reach a particular grade, we expect them to be able to do [these specific things] and demonstrate that they can [use this specific information or knowledge]."

Under Title I of NCLB, all states are required to have one set of content and achievement standards in reading, math, and science. Most states have established content standards in other subject matter areas, such as social studies, history, physical health, or technology. Not every content standard has a corresponding achievement expectation, however.

Some standards are broad statements of learner goals (e.g., "becoming self-sufficient learners") while others are very specific about what students should be able to know and do in a particular subject matter area (e.g., "students will read grade-level text with both high accuracy and appropriate pacing, intonation, and expression").

Standards are important for several reasons. They are intended to create equity across schools and classrooms in that they define what all teachers should teach, in all schools across a state. Standards also define the content that will be assessed and for which schools will be held accountable. Finally, since teachers are expected to teach to the standards, curricular frameworks, goals, and materials (e.g., textbooks) are to be directly aligned with a state's standards.

Assessment. Under NCLB, states are required to have one set of assessments that measure student performance on their content standards. States must assess at least 95% of all students in three content areas: reading/language arts, math, and science. They must assess students each year in each of the subject areas in Grades 3–8 and once during Grades 9–12. States must also establish three levels of achievement: Basic, Proficient, and Advanced.

Since the grade-level assessments would not be appropriate for some students with disabilities, especially those with significant cognitive disabilities, both IDEA and NCLB allow states to create alternate assessments and alternate achievement standards. However, only a limited number of students (i.e., not more than 1%) made be held to these alternate standards. Alternate achievement standards define student performance that differs from a grade-level achievement standard in terms of complexity, but these achievement standards must be aligned with a state's regular academic content standards, promote access to the general education curriculum, and reflect high or challenging standards.

Accountability. New demands for educational accountability under NCLB have changed the consequences for schools and individual students. School- and system-level accountability has dramatically increased and is based almost entirely on student assessment results. There are two primary ways that schools are held accountable: through public reporting such as school report cards and through a complicated process referred to as Adequate Yearly Progress (AYP).

States must publicly report assessment results at the school, district, and state levels for each grade, subject, and level and must report scores separately by gender, race/ethnicity, and for students identified as low income, special education, and limited English proficiency. In addition, schools and districts must report on a number of other indicators, such as the numbers of teachers who are fully certified, student attendance, suspensions and expulsions, drop-out rates, and graduation. The purpose of these reports is to make the educational performance of schools as transparent as possible.

In addition to the public reports, states must set annual performance targets for students in each of the three subject areas for each grade level and subgroup. The annual targets represent the percentage of students in a grade and subgroup who must reach the Proficient and Advanced levels of achievement on the state assessment. The annual targets are reported as AYP and designed to keep all subgroups on track to reaching Proficient or Advanced by the 2013–2014 school year. Specific consequences are applied to any school that fails to meet its annual AYP target for any subgroup.

While NCLB only addresses school- and system-level accountability, at the student level, accountability may mean that test scores are linked to promotion from grade to grade or to high school graduation. For example, in 2003–2004, states had high school graduation exams, and most of these exams require high levels of knowledge.

Standards-driven reform has an overriding goal of achieving higher levels of student achievement in subject matter content among all students. Thus, students with disabilities more than ever before need to have access to the demanding standards-based curriculum and instruction.

THE LINK BETWEEN STANDARDS AND CURRICULUM

As general and special education teachers approach the challenge of helping all students achieve at higher levels, they need to have a thorough understanding of how to provide access to the standards as well as the link between content and achievement standards, curriculum, and what they teach day-to-day. Furthermore, teachers, parents, and other practitioners need to deeply understand how the standards and the general education curriculum relate to an individual student's IEP.

Dissecting the Standards

Keep in mind that the primary purpose of content and achievement standards is to focus classroom instruction. Thus, it is important for teachers to be able to thoroughly understand what knowledge, information, and processes are implied or embedded in content and achievement standards. One finding from research that we have conducted in schools across the country that have been implementing standards-driven curriculum is that special education teachers have tended to "add on" new content rather than refocus what they teach (McLaughlin, Henderson, & Rhim, 1997; McLaughlin, Nolet, Rhim, & Henderson, 1999). In other words, teachers often want to keep their favorite lessons, curriculum, and materials, as well as continue to use their "tried and true" instructional strategies. For instance, they continue teaching specific functional skills (e.g., teaching time or money, etc.) while they attempt to also teach new standards-based skills, such as using estimation in math or engaging in writing activities. Teachers often feel torn by competing priorities and frustrated by lack of time to "cover it all." As a result, their teaching is focused on a collection of splinter schools or loosely collected knowledge.

The first thing that teachers need to know is that individual content and achievement standards do not stand alone but are connected across grade levels. Knowing what standards come before and which come after is very important to understanding what to teach and when to teach it. Figures 1.1 and 1.2 provide examples of specific state preK–3 reading/language arts standards and Grades 6–8 math standards.

In the sample of state standards, there are obvious "strands" or specific knowledge that appears across grade levels. For example, phonics is taught at the preK–2 level but with different levels of knowledge requirements. The math standards provide another example wherein the specific knowledge requirements do not change across the grade levels, but the expectations for how students are to demonstrate that knowledge become more demanding and complex.

What should be clear is that the knowledge required at each grade builds on what comes before and influences what comes after. Decisions made to not teach a specific set of skills, concepts, or standards at a particular grade have implications for all future grades as teachers simply cannot pick and choose among the content standards.

Another important consideration regarding standards is the interaction between specific knowledge and processes. Most state standards emphasize applied problem solving and authentic knowledge. Teaching to these standards requires more active roles for students and less teacher-directed instruction. There is less rote skill development and more emphasis on students' understanding topics and actually being able to do something with the content. Furthermore, many of the standards cross subject areas, such as requiring students to apply math concepts and skills in science or being able to communicate in writing how they solved a problem. Teachers need to adjust their instructional strategies to the intended outcome of the standard. As an example, "describe how a change in one variable in a linear function affects the other variable in a table of values." What are students intended to know and be able to do after receiving instruction directed at this standard?

Differentiating Between Content and Achievement Standards

We have been talking about developing a deeper understanding of the content standards and how they define the intended knowledge, skills, and

Figure 1.1 General Reading Processes: Phonics

Students will apply their knowledge of letter-sound relationships and word structure to decode unfamiliar words.

Prekindergarten	***Kindergarten***	***Grade 1***	***Grade 2***	***Grade 3***
Phonics	*Phonics*	*Phonics*	*Phonics*	*Phonics*
Decode words in grade-level texts	Decode words in grade-level texts	Decode words in grade-level texts	Decode words in grade-level texts	Decode words in grade-level texts
Identify and name some upper- and lowercase letters in words, especially those in the student's own name	Identify similarities and differences in letters and words	Recognize and apply short vowels, long vowels, and *y* as a vowel	Use phonics to decode words	Sound out common word parts
	Blend letter sounds in one-syllable words (CVC)	Decode words with letter combinations, such as consonant digraphs, blends, and special vowel patterns	Break compound words, contractions, and inflectional endings into known parts	Break words into familiar parts
	Use onset and rime (word families) to decode one-syllable words	Read one-syllable words fluently (CVC, CVCE)	Identify and apply vowel patterns to read words, such as CVC, CVCE, CVVC	Use word meanings and order in sentences to confirm decoding efforts
		Use known word/part to decode unknown words, such as car → card	Read blends fluently, such as *spl*, *str*	

Figure 1.2 Standard 1.0: Knowledge of Algebra, Patterns, or Functions

Students will algebraically represent, model, analyze, or solve mathematical or real-world problems involving patterns or functional relationships.

Grade 6	*Grade 7*	*Grade 8*
A. Patterns and Functions	A. Patterns and Functions	A. Patterns and Functions
1. Identify, describe, extend, and create numeric patterns and functions (a) Identify and describe sequences represented by a physical model or in a function table (b) Interpret and write a rule for a one-operation (+, −, ×, ÷) function table (c) Complete a function table with a two-operation rule	1. Identify, describe, extend, and create linear patterns and functions (a) Identify and extend an arithmetic sequence represented as a function table (b) Identify and extend a geometric sequence (c) Describe how a change in one variable in a linear function affects the other variable in a table of values	1. Identify, describe, extend, and create patterns, functions, and sequences (a) Determine the recursive relationship of arithmetic sequences represented in words, in a table, or in a graph (b) Determine the recursive relationship of geometric sequences represented in words, in a table, or in a graph (c) Determine whether functions are linear or nonlinear when represented in words, in a table, symbolically, or in a graph (d) Determine whether functions are linear or nonlinear when represented symbolically

processes. In contrast, achievement standards define how well or how proficiently students must demonstrate the knowledge, skills, and processes. Achievement standards are typically defined by the assessments, which should be clearly aligned with the standards. However, assessments cannot measure every aspect of every standard, so assessments are designed to sample student performance.

State assessments, often referred to as "large-scale" assessments can give teachers important information about the general grade level at which a student is performing. Also, unlike older forms of multiple-choice assessments, the newer assessments are designed to illustrate the processes and applications that are intended by the content standards.

As you can see from the sample items in Figures 1.3 and 1.4, today's assessments include both traditional multiple choice test items as well as constructed response items, which require that students explain answers or processes or expand on specific items. Conventional essay questions are also included. The items model the types of instruction that is expected and the skills and processes in the standards. Teachers are supposed to teach to these tests! However, large-scale assessments are not designed to provide the breadth or depth of information about a student's level of understanding in a standard area and cannot be the sole source of information used for developing instructional units, lesson plans, or IEPs.

Figure 1.3 Examples of Fourth-Grade Math Assessment Items

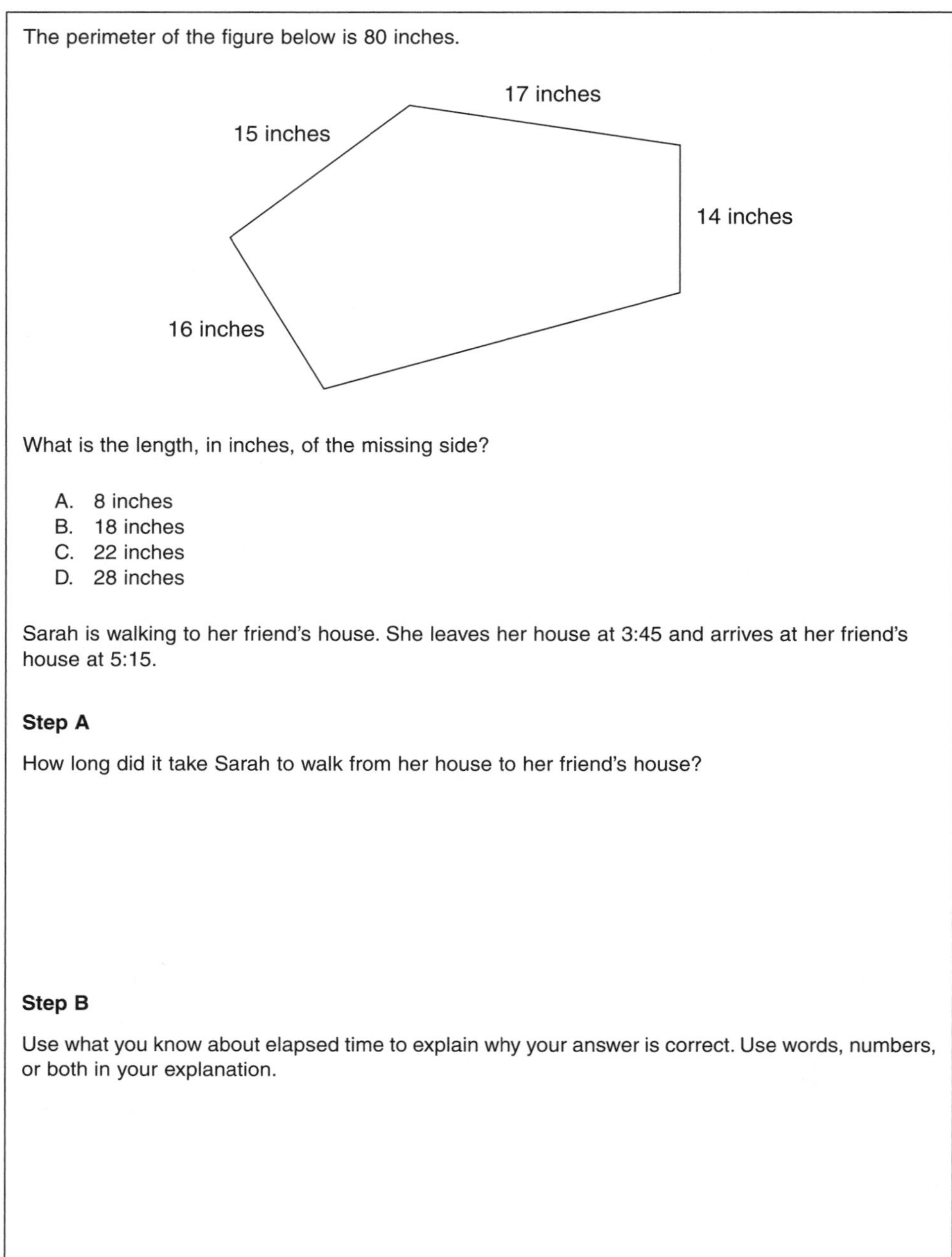

The perimeter of the figure below is 80 inches.
17 inches
15 inches
14 inches
16 inches
What is the length, in inches, of the missing side?
A. 8 inches
B. 18 inches
C. 22 inches
D. 28 inches
Sarah is walking to her friend's house. She leaves her house at 3:45 and arrives at her friend's house at 5:15.
Step A
How long did it take Sarah to walk from her house to her friend's house?
Step B
Use what you know about elapsed time to explain why your answer is correct. Use words, numbers, or both in your explanation.

Standards and Curriculum

By now, you know that standards are intended to drive the curriculum. In the next chapter, you will learn a great deal more about what constitutes "curriculum" and how to find the "general education curriculum." Before you do that, it is important to find out more about the curriculum that is used in your

Figure 1.4 Grade 8 Reading Assessment

Choose the word or group of words that means the same, or about the same, as the underlined word. Then mark the space with the answer you have chosen.

A spike is like a ______.

A. brick
B. pillow
C. dish
D. nail

Read the story "Arachne" and "Damon and Pythias" and answer the following question.

By allowing Pythias to settle his affairs, Dionysus shows that he can be:

A. brave
B. compassionate
C. indifferent
D. indecisive

Read the story "Wang Yani" and answer the following question.

What advice would Yani probably give to young people? Use details from the story to support your answer.

Write your answer on your answer document.

school or district. Many districts and states have developed K–12 curriculum in content areas that align with their state standards. However, not all districts have such an aligned curriculum. So, it is important that you get a copy of your state's standards and then compare them to whatever curriculum guides exist in your district. Don't forget to examine important curriculum materials such as textbooks. These should also reflect or align with the standards. This activity is something that faculty within an entire school or grade level might need to engage in.

Among the things that you and your colleagues should identify as you investigate your state's standards are the specific topics covered within a subject matter domain. For example, in the standards in Figure 1.2, mathematics in Grades 6–8 covers the same algebraic topics of patterns and functions. Note the changes in the standards from Grade 6, "identify and describe sequences represented by a physical model or in a function table," Grade 7, "identify and extend an arithmetic sequence represented as a function table," and Grade 8, "determine the recursive relationship of arithmetic sequences represented in words, in a table or in a graph." Which main topics does your math curriculum cover across the grade levels?

You should also dig deeper into each of the specific topics to examine the specific skills and types of processes that are included. For example, which computation skills are addressed at which grade levels? What about application of knowledge and skills? What are students expected to be able to do or demonstrate? Are these taught at all grades? Sometimes standards can be overly general and not provide the level of detail necessary to do such a comparison. In that case, you may need to talk to an outside curriculum expert from your district or state to determine exactly what is expected in the standard.

Of course, you should also become very familiar with your state's assessments. The result of this investigation will be a better understanding of what skills are likely to be addressed at specific grade levels. Remember, you can't just focus on the grade(s) you teach, but you must look at what comes before and what will come after. After all of this analysis, you are likely to find some areas that you have ignored in your instruction as well as things you have been teaching that are not reflected in the standards. This may mean changing what and how you teach. It can mean eliminating some content, or it can also mean finding ways to incorporate the standards into specific instructional units or lessons that you do teach.

Also, don't forget to examine your textbooks, reading series, and other curriculum materials. Sometimes textbooks can contradict specific standards, or they may not emphasize certain skills. You need to make sure that you use textbooks and other materials that support the goals of the state standards.

One strategy that can be particularly useful in helping teachers better understand how standards translate into instruction is to examine student work. After teachers understand what is expected, they can jointly identify and discuss evidence of the standards within student papers or other assignments. Students can also be asked to explain. This helps teachers gain a deeper awareness of what a specific standard looks like in practice.

Standards and Students With Disabilities

Standards have had a particular impact on students with disabilities. First, there is increasing evidence that standards are resulting in higher expectations and higher levels of achievement among students with disabilities (McLaughlin et al., in press; Nagle, 2004).

However, teachers face a number of challenges in their efforts to provide students with disabilities access to standards. One challenge, which we discussed earlier in this chapter, is the limited amount of time that is available to teach all of the skills that teachers believe students with disabilities need to learn. The pace of instruction has increased in general education classrooms due to the amount of content that is expected to be covered under the state standards, so there is less time to support students who may require more time or have a lesson taught differently or be given more opportunity to practice skills.

For a student who has skill deficits, the challenge is often how to teach the specific skills and also allow the student to keep up with the grade-level curriculum. Helping students with disabilities succeed in a standards-driven curriculum requires that teachers know the core and essential knowledge embedded in content standards and how to assess where a student is performing with respect to that core knowledge. In the following chapters, you will learn how to do all of these things. But, before you begin to focus on an individual student, let's take a final look at the big picture of how state standards, coupled with the emphasis on accountability, is changing how we think about special education.

A NEW WAY TO THINK ABOUT SPECIAL EDUCATION

The foundation of special education rests with the guarantee that each eligible student receives a "free and appropriate public education" or FAPE. What is appropriate for an individual student is to be determined by parents and a multidisciplinary team of professionals. These decisions are evident in a student's IEP, which specifies the annual educational goals and the special education and related services that a student requires to meet those goals.

The traditional model of developing IEPs and of designing special education viewed students with disabilities in isolation of broader general education curricular goals. Children were tested; their learning strengths and deficits were identified; and individual goals, objectives, and strategies were devised to meet the deficits. Educational evaluations were typically conducted in isolation from the larger general education curriculum and focused on discrete skill deficits. IEPs often were a collection of isolated skill objectives that led to isolated instruction (Shriner & DeStefano, 2003). A student's program may have been individualized, but it was based on annual goals and thus separated from the scope and sequence of a curriculum. Often, the IEP became *the* curriculum for a student.

Within the standards-driven reform model, special education is evolving into an array of services and supports that provide a student access to the general education curriculum, and the IEP becomes a tool that specifies how to implement general education curriculum with an individual student.

The new model of special education is illustrated in Figure 1.5.

In this model, a student's IEP is based on an assessment that indicates where a student is functioning (e.g., at what level is the student's knowledge, skills, and processes within specific subject matter) within the general education

Figure 1.5 Special Education and the General Curriculum

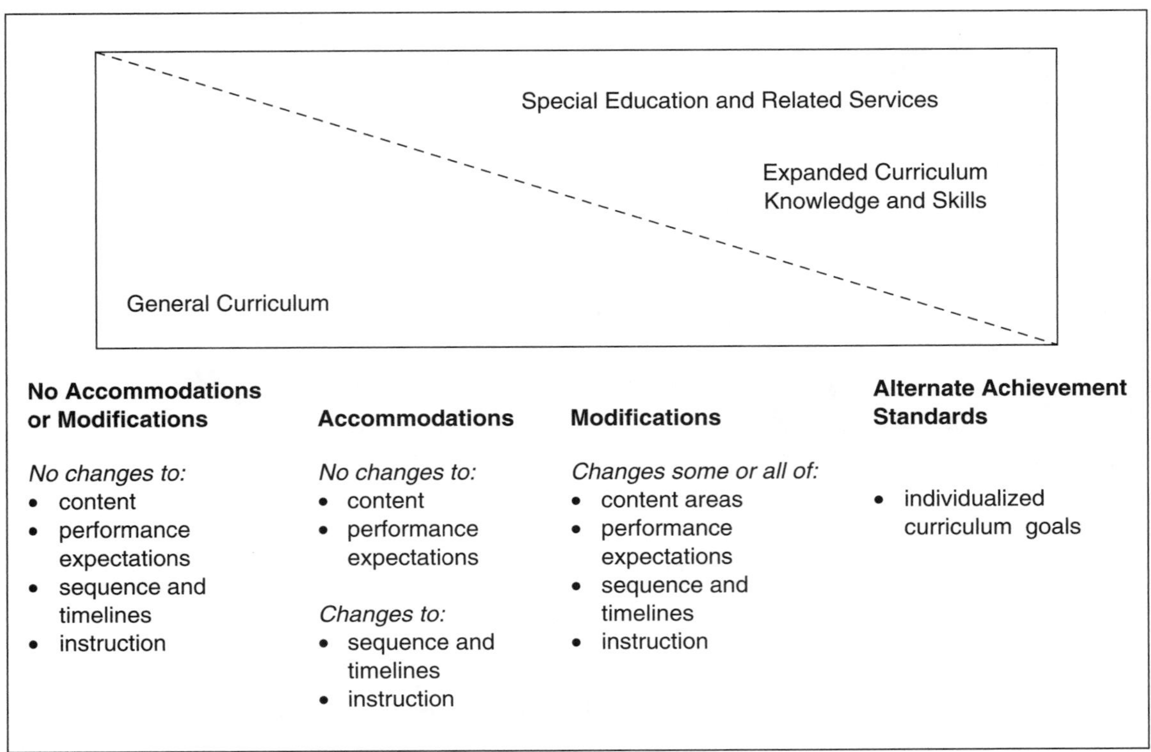

curriculum, which reflects the standards. The goals for special education instruction as well as the accommodations and services and supports required to help the student access and progress in the curriculum are also specified. The IEP should address how special education will supplement the general education curriculum by providing instruction in specific curricular areas or skill areas not addressed in the general education curriculum. Decisions about an IEP are individualized, but they start from the expectation that the student is to learn the general education curriculum, and special education's role is to help the student learn and progress in that curriculum. We will provide much more information about the IEP in Chapter 6.

Challenges for Special and General Education Teachers

There are a number of challenges facing all teachers as they implement standards, assessments, and accountability reforms with students with disabilities. The most significant of these challenges is how to enable each student to access the critical knowledge and skills specified in the standards. The stakes for schools and for students are higher than ever. If students do not have meaningful access to the general education curriculum, they cannot be expected to become proficient on state and local assessments. Poor performance on these assessments can lead to consequences for schools. What is more, consequences for students are also increasing. Students who do not do well in the general education curriculum may not be promoted from one grade to another or receive a high school diploma.

Access to the general education curriculum must become the cornerstone of a student's IEP and define the special education and related services that will be provided. These changes to the IEP will require changes to special education instruction and the organization of special education in the schools. To provide access will require much more of special education teachers.

The quick fixes and simplistic approaches have already been tried and rejected. Providing access to the general education curriculum will require a new way of thinking about both special education and individual students with disabilities. Teaching that ensures that all students have access to the general education curriculum will involve having knowledge of subject matter content, processes involved in learning, and strategies for designing instruction. Teaching that ensures access to the general curriculum requires an integrated understanding of the separate and combined effects of all three of these domains in the teaching and learning process.

This book is designed to help you integrate these three domains of knowledge to ensure that all students have meaningful access to the general education curriculum. In Chapter 2, you will learn about curriculum. We will examine what the general education curriculum really is and how it influences what happens day-to-day in a classroom. In Chapter 3, we will discuss the recent research on human learning and the implications of this research for designing effective instruction. New ideas about learning underlie much of the school reform movement and are beginning to have a profound effect on every aspect of schooling. We will discuss the teaching implications of this research and provide you with a rationale for making instructional design decisions that match student learning. In Chapter 4, we will discuss assessment strategies to help you know when a student is succeeding in the general curriculum as well as how to monitor their progress. In Chapter 5, we will discuss how to plan instruction that is accessible for all students, and we will describe the continuum of supports that creates access to the general curriculum. In Chapter 6, we will provide strategies for developing an IEP that provides access to the general education curriculum. Finally, in the Appendix, we have provided a list of resources for teachers and administrators seeking additional information about some of the issues we discuss in the book.

As you will see, the challenge of making the general education curriculum accessible for all students requires a new way of thinking and problem solving. This is not a "how-to" book. It is a "how to think" book. We hope that it will stimulate conversations and actions in your own school that enable you to find new ways to be effective with all of your students.

The Nature of Curriculum

Curriculum is at the center of standards-based reform because it is through curriculum that students are provided the opportunity to learn the intended content and achieve the standards. Surprisingly little agreement exists among educators about the exact meaning of *curriculum*. For example, over 1,100 curriculum books were written during the 20th century, and each offered its own variation on the meaning of the term (Cuban, 1993). Curriculum is the "what" and "how" of schooling. Traditionally, curriculum has referred to any educational program lasting for several years, such as the courses taught in college and university programs or public schools. Public school practitioners often narrow the meaning of curriculum to refer only to materials used in the classroom, such as textbooks. Meanwhile, curriculum theorists often use the term more broadly to refer to the full range of experiences that students undertake under the guidance of schools. All of these interpretations of curriculum can be found in schools today, and sometimes the precise interpretation of the term can only be derived from the context in which it is used.

In this chapter, we will examine the characteristics of public school K–12 curriculum, with particular attention to the general curriculum. As you will see, curriculum is complex and multifaceted. We believe that to truly understand what it means to access the general curriculum, you need to understand how curriculum works.

MULTIPLE TYPES OF CURRICULUM

The first thing to understand about curriculum is that it can have different meanings, depending on the perspective from which it is viewed. Often, these different meanings are referred to as *types* of curriculum. The three types of curriculum most pertinent to our discussion here are the *intended* curriculum, the *taught* curriculum, and the *learned* curriculum (Cuban, 1993).

The Intended Curriculum

The *intended curriculum* is the official or adopted curriculum, often contained in state or district policy. This is the body of content that students are expected to learn as a result of their school experiences. Intended curricula generally take the form of formal, written documents that reflect the educational theory and societal values that prevail at a given time. The various curriculum frameworks currently in use in many of the United States are prime examples of intended curricula. Most state curriculum frameworks include broad descriptions of subject matter content domains and often specify the benchmarks and objectives students would be expected to meet at a specific grade level. There can be little doubt that the policymakers who formulate these curricula, and by extension, the public these individuals represent, intend that these curriculum frameworks will be the basis of instruction delivered in local schools. Indeed, many state and district assessments and school accountability measures are linked directly to the goals, objectives, and benchmarks contained in the intended curriculum.

In addition to the curriculum frameworks associated with specific content standards, state departments of education routinely specify what subjects students must take. This has been particularly true at middle and high school levels, where the intended curriculum often takes the form of graduation credit requirements.

Sometimes, standards set by professional or certifying organizations constitute an intended curriculum. For example, schools offering an International Baccalaureate High School diploma follow a highly prescribed curriculum (Laurent-Brennan, 1998). When the intended curriculum is developed at the local level, it can be narrowly defined and may pertain to supplementary subject areas such as health or physical education.

Although the Individualized Education Program (IEP) developed for a particular student who receives special education specifies the goals and objectives a student is expected to meet, the IEP is not an intended curriculum for that student. Rather, the IEP is a plan for making the intended curriculum more immediate and specific for the student. The goals and objectives on a student's IEP should supplement, as well as support, the intended curriculum but not replace it.

The Taught Curriculum

The *taught curriculum* is the operationalization of the intended curriculum. The taught curriculum involves the minute-to-minute, day-to-day, and week-to-week events that actually occur in the classroom or other instructional settings. However, the taught curriculum is more than just lessons and activities. It includes teacher instructional behaviors, such as questioning or lecturing, and other instructional variables, such as time allocated for instruction, grouping arrangements, classroom rules, and materials. The taught curriculum also includes less formal aspects of teaching, such as incidental comments or conversations, as well as the teacher beliefs and attitudes as they pertain to the intended curriculum. Sometimes, these informal, unplanned events are what are most salient for students, as the situation in Box 2.1 illustrates.

Box 2.1 Mr. Painter Teaches About the Nile

Sometimes, the taught curriculum has unintended side effects.

Mr. Painter's middle school class was engaged in a world geography lesson about Egypt. Instruction consisted of students taking turns reading aloud from their textbook round-robin style. While one student read aloud, the rest of the students followed along in their own books. Every once in a while, Mr. Painter would comment on the reading to help make the activity more interesting for the students. Following a passage that presented the fact, "The longest river in Egypt is the Nile," the teacher made the following comment:

"Thank you, Mandy. Class, if you ever go to Egypt, don't stick your hand in the Nile because they have a little snail that lives there that can get into your skin and make you very sick. The disease you can get is called *schistosomiasis*. Schistosomiasis is a bad disease. You don't want to get it. Okay Phillip, it's your turn to read."

Phillip then read the next paragraph in the text. The students in the class continued studying Egypt for the next 3 days. During that time, they read about the pyramids and mummies, looked at maps, completed a set of worksheets about the climate of North Africa, and watched a documentary about the Suez Canal. At no time during those 3 days was schistosomiasis ever mentioned or even alluded to again. On the fourth day after the Nile River lesson, the students were asked to write a brief essay about the most important things they had learned about Egypt and North Africa.

Out of 25 students in the class, 22 mentioned schistosomiasis or made some reference to a snail that lives in the Nile and causes illness. A total of 8 students *only* discussed schistosomiasis in their essays, to the exclusion of all other topics addressed during the week. Only 2 of the students mentioned pyramids, and none mentioned the Suez Canal. The students had been exposed to nearly 5 hours of instruction about Egypt, distributed over 4 days, yet the thing they most often remembered and to which they attached importance was a passing 10-second comment from the teacher.

The taught curriculum also includes curriculum materials such as textbooks, worksheets, and electronic media with which students interact. Although many teachers refer to curriculum materials such as textbooks as "the curriculum," this is a misnomer. Materials, no matter how well organized or how detailed, do not constitute a curriculum. Curriculum materials do exert a strong influence on the instruction that takes place in classrooms; however, there is considerable variation in teachers' use of curriculum materials (Stodolsky, 1989). Curriculum materials, particularly textbooks, may affect what topics or activities teachers choose to teach in areas such as reading and math (Freeman & Porter, 1989), but textbooks are not a proxy for the taught curriculum. Teachers may exercise wide latitude in variables such as how topics get covered, how much time is allocated to a topic, the kinds of activities and lessons that get used, and how students will be asked to use the information taught. Content and performance standards may tend to reduce such variability across teachers, classrooms, and schools.

Historically, for many children who receive special education, the IEP becomes the taught curriculum. That is, their entire educational program or program within a specific subject matter area is comprised of the specific goals and objectives contained on their IEP (Pugach & Warger, 1993). This has the same effect as textbooks, which is a drastic narrowing of the curriculum for these individuals. When the IEP is the taught curriculum, goals tend to be shortsighted and fragmented, with little linkage to larger or longer term outcomes.

The Learned Curriculum

The *learned curriculum* is what students actually learn as a result of being in the classroom and interacting with the intended and taught curriculum. The learned curriculum includes the skills and knowledge that generally are associated with school learning as well as a wide variety of other information that may or may not be part of the intended or taught curricula. For example, a negative attitude about math may be learned from a teacher who models such an attitude, or students who experience repeated school failure may learn "helplessness."

The problem for teachers is that what their students learn may not be what they taught or what they intended them to learn. Most of the time, most students learn most of what their teachers expect them to learn. However, for some, the learned curriculum may include inaccuracies, misconceptions, and incomplete information. The only way we can ever know what it is students really have learned is to ask them to demonstrate it. Unfortunately, our inferences about what students learn are only as accurate as our assessment procedures, and many classroom testing procedures provide very poor information about the learned curriculum. One of the aims of alternate assessments such as performance tasks and portfolios is to create more contextually relevant situations in which students can fully demonstrate what they have learned.

THE CORE ELEMENTS OF CURRICULUM

As you can see, it is important to be clear about the type of curriculum (intended, taught, or learned) to which you are referring. Different aspects of curriculum may appear to be more or less dominant, depending on the context you are considering. However, there are three interrelated aspects of curriculum that cut across all of the three types we discussed. These aspects underlie most of the decisions you will make about curriculum:

1. Curriculum has a purpose. Curriculum is planned and is linked to desired outcomes. These outcomes may be broadly defined (e.g., prepare effective citizens) or they may be very specific (e.g., teach children in the third grade to write in cursive).

2. Curriculum involves a domain. A domain is an identifiable body of information related to a particular knowledge or skill area. Specification of the domain defines the limits of what is and is not part of the curriculum.

3. Curriculum involves time. There are two ways curriculum is affected by time: the time allocated for various topics and activities, and the sequence in which information is taught and learned.

WHAT IS THE PURPOSE OF CURRICULUM?

Curriculum is not simply the stream of events and activities or lessons that occur in a classroom or school. Rather, curriculum is an interrelated set of plans and activities that occur across grades and are intended to result in identifiable *outcomes* that almost always pertain to student learning (Marsh & Willis, 1995). Sometimes these outcomes (or goals) are stated explicitly, as in the case of content and performance standards listed in state or district frameworks. Other times, curricular goals are simply implied by a teacher's choice of materials or allocation of instructional time.

It is important to remember that curriculum is intended to benefit individual students as well as the greater society in which those students operate. For example, social studies was introduced as a distinct content area during the early part of the 20th century when education was intended to promote the assimilation of a rapidly growing population that included large numbers of children from rural and immigrant families arriving in the industrial cities. Schools were expected to prepare effective citizens who could take their place as productive members of the American workforce. Similarly, science and math curriculum frequently were scrutinized and reformed in the 1950s and 1960s when it was believed the United States was lagging behind the Soviet Union in the cold war and ensuing space race. Today, standards-based school reform clearly is expected to result in benefits for society by producing workers who will be able to contribute to a 21st-century global economy.

Teachers tend to have a very specific view of curriculum and are used to thinking about curriculum in the context of their classrooms or students. Teachers are primarily concerned with how or what to teach today, this week, and this year. This more immediate perspective results in shorter term goals and objectives. Indeed, some of the tension that has formed around standards-based reform, particularly in the context of special education, is that it is sometimes difficult for teachers to see the benefits for individual students in content and performance standards that may appear to be too academic or cognitively demanding, or teachers don't see the link between what they are accustomed to teaching and the content standards or achievement standards. Yet, despite the short-term difficulties involved in teaching these skills, these larger goals may be very important to lifelong success. One of the most important purposes of curriculum is to serve as a map that provides information about short-term goals as well as long-term outcomes.

Curriculum as a Map for Teachers

When you use a map to plan a road trip, you always have your eventual destination in mind, but you can't simply draw a straight line from point A to point B. You have to take into account variables such as the location of the specific roads on which you will be traveling, how fast you can travel, and the overall distance you will be covering. Often, you identify interim landmarks that help you decide whether you are on the right track.

You can use this same kind of thinking to connect the shorter term goals for an individual to broader curriculum outcomes. Two things teachers must consider in using curriculum this way are *immediacy* and *specificity.*

Immediacy

Immediacy refers to the settings and time frame in which a curriculum outcome is expected to occur. Immediate environments are those in which students are expected to operate frequently, such as their classrooms, playgrounds, or homes. Less immediate environments are those in which the student is exposed to only occasionally or those in which a student is expected to perform in the future, such as next year's math class, after graduation from high school, or in the workplace. It is important to remember that most district or state content standards are intended to reflect learning that has occurred over multiple years. These standards are frequently broken down into smaller annual objectives or benchmarks and often correspond to when assessments are administered.

As you think about the purpose of curriculum outcomes or goals for a particular individual or class, you must consider how soon you expect the outcome to occur. For special education teachers, that means planning for the immediate classroom environments and current instructional units or lesson plans as well as for the next several years, such as when a key transition occurs (i.e., elementary to middle school, middle to high school, and adulthood). There should be a clear path from the immediate, short-term goals that apply in today's class to the long-term goals you would want the student to accomplish in the content domain.

Specificity

The purpose of curriculum is to direct classroom instruction. Some curriculum goals are very focused, for example, requiring students to learn a specific skill such as "single-digit multiplication." A more diffuse goal may be for students to learn to "understand and apply concepts and procedures from number sense." Special education IEP goals tend to be fairly specific, while content standards in most statewide curriculum frameworks tend to be more general. As a rule, the more specific a curriculum outcome is, the more easily it can be broken into teachable steps that can be measured. Yet, if we only focus on small steps, we lose the larger focus and the ability to do long-term planning. In other words, it is important not to lose sight of the forest because of the trees. Many states, in their standards development, have attempted to reach a middle ground between highly specific, observable goals that are readily teachable and the more general statements of outcomes. For example, Kansas uses the descriptors associated with its science standards shown in Figure 2.1.

Figure 2.1 Kansas Science Standards

Standards: General statements of what students should know, understand, and be able to do in the natural sciences over the course of their K–12 education. The standards are interwoven ideas, not separate entities; thus, they should be taught as interwoven ideas, not as separate entities. Science standards for the state of Kansas are clustered for Grade levels K–2, 3–4, 5–8, and 9–12:

1. Science as Inquiry
2. Physical Science
3. Life Science
4. Earth and Space Science
5. Science and Technology
6. Science in Personal and Environmental Perspectives
7. History and Nature of Science

Here is the Science as Inquiry standard:

> *As a result of the activities in grades K–2, all students should experience science as full inquiry. In elementary grades, students begin to develop the physical and intellectual abilities of scientific inquiry.*

Benchmarks: Specific statements of what students should know and be able to do at a specified point in their schooling. Benchmarks are used to measure students' progress toward meeting a standard. Benchmarks for the Kansas science standards are defined for grades 2, 4, 8, and 10.

Here is the first Benchmark for the Science as Inquiry standard:

> *All students will begin to develop abilities necessary to do scientific inquiries. However, not every activity will involve all of these stages nor must any particular sequences of these stages be followed. Full inquiry involves asking a simple question, completing an investigation, answering the question, and presenting the results to others.*

Indicators: Statements of the knowledge or skills which students demonstrate in order to meet a benchmark. Indicators are critical to understanding the standards and benchmarks and are to be met by all students. For the Kansas science standards, the indicators listed under each benchmark are not listed in priority order, nor should the list be considered as all-inclusive. The list of indicators and examples should be considered as representative but not comprehensive or all-inclusive.

Examples: Two kinds of examples are used in the Kansas science standards. An instructional example offers an activity or a specific concrete instance of an idea of what is called for by an indicator. A clarifying example provides an illustration of the meaning or intent of an indicator. Like the indicators themselves, examples are considered to be representative but not comprehensive or all-inclusive.

Here are Indicators and Examples for the Science as Inquiry Benchmark presented above:

Indicator: *The student will identify characteristics of objects.*
Example: *The student states characteristics of leaves, shells, water, and air.*
Indicator: *The student will classify and arrange groups of objects by a variety of characteristics.*
Example: *The student groups seeds by color, texture, size; groups objects by whether they float or sink; groups rocks by texture, color, and hardness.*

CURRICULUM INVOLVES A DOMAIN

Curriculum is the "what" of schooling; it is the content that teachers teach and that students learn. Curriculum is separate from the strategies teachers use to manage and instruct students in the content (i.e., methods) although the line between curriculum and instruction often is (and should be) difficult to separate in day-to-day practice. The extent or breadth of specific curriculum content (also called *scope*) is determined by the nature of the subject matter domain (e.g., earth science, consumer mathematics, writing) and the purpose of the curriculum (e.g., teach basic skills, teach authentic use of knowledge such as algebra).

When the skills and knowledge are defined broadly, or when the purpose is ill defined, the scope will be less clear. Narrower domains and well-defined purposes generally will limit the scope of a curriculum. For example, the scope of a curriculum intended to "promote moral development" likely would be much broader and less well defined than that of a curriculum intended to prepare commercial refrigeration technicians. The scope is a horizontal look at the range of courses, topics, or activities within a subject matter across a given time frame or grade level, or across a given student's educational career. A third-grade math curriculum might present a range of topics including single- and two-digit addition, subtraction with regrouping, single-digit multiplication, two-step word problems, proportion, probability, and measurement. These topics would not necessarily all be treated equally during the third grade year, though. Some would be taught to mastery while others might only be introduced. However, each probably would be addressed in some way at some point during the third-grade year.

Specifying the Domain

The information that makes up curriculum comes in a variety of forms. A number of taxonomies have been suggested over the years to describe the types of information in school curricula, including the well-known ones formulated by Bloom (Bloom, Engelhart, Furst, Hill, & Krathwohl, 1956) and Gagne (1974). In general, information in curriculum takes the form of facts, concepts, principles, and procedures. Descriptions of these are shown in Figure 2.2.

There are two reasons why it is critical for teachers to understand the underlying structure of the information contained in curriculum. First, teachers must design instruction that matches as closely as possible the cognitive processes involved in learning the subject matter. In the next chapter, we will examine those processes, and as you will see, the learning processes depend greatly on the type of information to be learned. For example, recall of facts involves a different kind of thinking than application of a strategy. Because different kinds of information are learned and remembered differently, they also must be taught differently.

Therefore, the success a student experiences in learning the information contained in curriculum depends, to a great extent, on the teacher's ability to match specific instructional strategies with the content and the purpose or goal of learning that content.

Figure 2.2 Types of Information Found in the Curriculum

Facts are defined as simple associations between names, objects, events, places, and so on that use singular exemplars. Learning facts involves making a consistent connection between a stimulus and a response. This association may simply involve associating a label or name with an object, or it may express a relationship between two or more objects or events, for example, the phrase "Salem is the capital of Oregon." Because facts describe only one relationship, they may be grouped together in descriptions of unique events, objects, or places. In a chapter in a world geography textbook, a section describing the Indian subcontinent might include specific facts about climate and topography grouped together under the subtitle, "Four Greats of India" (great rivers, great winds, great mountains, and the great plateau). However, each individual fact (e.g., the name of each of the rivers or the location of the great plateau) would need to be taught and remembered as a specific name or place. In this respect, facts may not be difficult to teach or test, but they are especially difficult to learn because they must be memorized and have little explanatory power beyond the specific stimulus-response relationship they describe.

Concepts are clusters of events, names, dates, objects, places, and so forth that share a common set of defining attributes or characteristics. A concept may be thought of as a category having a rule that defines its relevant characteristics, a name, and a set of instances or exemplars that share the key attributes. In this definition, rules provide the basis for organizing the attributes of the concept; these attributes, in turn, provide the criteria for distinguishing examples of the concept from nonexamples. This is a classical view of concepts that does not cover every contingency likely to be encountered, but it does provide a framework for thinking about content contained in the curriculum. Many concepts encountered in content classes are quite complex, with conditional or nested attributes, or membership in multiple categories.

Principles indicate causal or covariant relationships among different facts or concepts, more often the latter. A principle usually represents an if-then or cause-effect relationship, although this relationship may not be stated explicitly. A principle generally involves multiple applications in which the fundamental relationship among the relevant concepts is constant across virtually all examples of the concepts. For example, the law of supply and demand may be taught as the principle, "When supply goes up, demand goes down," with comparable applications found in the context of medieval European city states, a child's lemonade stand, and the 1929 stock market crash.

Procedures involve the steps or phases required to complete a process. For example, the topic "Scientific Method" may be taught in seventh-grade science class as a series of steps proceeding from formation of a hypothesis, construction of an experiment, collection of data, and evaluation of results. However, procedural knowledge involves more than simply knowing what the steps are, but focuses on knowing how to execute those steps in an actual experiment. Often, procedures can be formatted as a set of principles that comprise a decision chain of the form, "If A occurs, then I do B; if C occurs, then I do D, and so on," with execution following a series of decisions based on results obtained at each preceding step. For example, writing a research paper might involve a series of decisions about where to obtain information, which information to include, the order in which information should be presented, and so on.

The second reason it is important for teachers to understand the type of the information contained in the curriculum is that the types of information students learn determines the kind of thinking they can do. The more complex the information, the more useful it is for higher order thinking and problem solving. These require different types of instruction. Unfortunately, much of what students traditionally have been asked to learn in schools is comprised primarily of facts and simple concepts. However, as we noted in Chapter 1, many of the new standards and curriculum in place in schools today require more complex learning. One of the biggest challenges teachers face is to help their students transform facts and simple concepts into principles and procedures. Specifying the domain of the general curriculum involves a process of cataloging the types of information involved (facts, concepts, principles, procedures) and then prioritizing that information in order of importance for accomplishing desired outcomes. This prioritization process should be based on teacher domain expertise as well as the specificity and immediacy of expected outcomes.

CURRICULUM AND TIME

It is impossible to think about curriculum without thinking about time. Two dimensions of time are of particular concern. The first has to do with the allocation of instructional or learning time to various aspects of the curriculum, and the second has to do with the order in which a curriculum presents information and activities over time.

Allocated Time

Allocated time is the time a district, school, or teacher provides for instruction (Berliner, 1990). Time allocated to instruction should be distinguished from *engaged time,* which is the time students actually spend paying attention to materials or activities that have educational goals. While time allocated may not necessarily translate directly to engaged time, it is a reasonable indicator of the extent to which students have the opportunity to learn in a particular domain. Needless to say, students whose opportunities to receive instruction in a curriculum area are limited because too little time is allocated for instruction would be unlikely to meet challenging performance standards in that area.

Allocated time has additional meaning when we consider students who have learning problems. If our expectation is that a student is going to *attain* a particular curricular goal, rather than simply receive instruction related to it, then we need to ensure that sufficient time is allocated for learning to occur. Of course, all other things being equal, students who have learning problems require more time to learn than their typical same age peers. It may be difficult to make the claim that a student who has learning problems has had an *adequate* opportunity to learn if insufficient time is allocated to accommodate her or his specific learning needs.

Time allocated to various aspects of the curriculum generally reflects an ordering of instructional priorities. More time usually is allocated to those curriculum areas that are of higher priority to a district, school, or teacher. For example, in elementary school, a large proportion of the day is allocated to reading and writing instruction because learning to read and write are viewed as the most important outcomes for students at that level. In later grades, more time is allocated to other topics as the focus shifts from basic skills to more subject matter content instruction.

Two common problems associated with prioritizing curriculum are *overload* and *omission.* When the scope of the curriculum is too wide (i.e., we try to squeeze too much information into the curriculum), students do not have enough time to master much, if any, of the content. This is an overloaded curriculum. Curriculum that suffer from this problem often are described as being a mile wide and an inch deep. There are many topics, but little depth or mastery of subject matter. This is a problem of many curriculum programs used in the

United States. In an attempt to be all things to all users, textbooks often include far too much information about a given topic. Teachers who fail to make thoughtful choices about which aspects of the subject matter to address may end up overloading the curriculum. The chief dilemma resulting from this problem is the lack of instructional time available to help students learn the material. Teachers often are reduced to simply mentioning or glossing over subject matter.

The second problem involves curriculum omissions. Keep in mind that there is a finite amount of time available in a school year, so each time teachers make the decision to include or emphasize some piece of information, they also make an implicit decision not to include other things. For example, if over the course of a year-long sixth-grade language arts class, a teacher spends relatively more instructional time teaching a generic writing process, relatively little time may be allocated to instruction on strategies for writing research papers. If students never have the opportunity to learn how to write research papers, omission of this skill from the curriculum will be problematic later on when more technical writing is required.

Curriculum Sequence

Sequence refers to the order in which a curriculum presents information and activities over time, either within or across school years. Knowing how a particular curriculum is sequenced can help teachers avoid the problems of curriculum overload or curriculum omission. Teachers must establish priorities about what to include in the curriculum. There are a number of organizing strategies that can be used to sequence curriculum information (Armstrong, 1989; Posner & Strike, 1976; Smith & Ragan, 2005). Here are some commonly used sequencing strategies:

Thematic Sequencing. Topics are organized so that skills and knowledge associated with separate themes are taught together. For example, a middle school general science class might include the separate themes of *electricity and magnetism, plate tectonics, ecology,* and *human systems.* With thematic sequencing, each thematic unit stands alone. Knowing the information associated with one theme may not lead to a better understanding of the next theme to be taught. For example, knowing how *s waves* and *p waves* function in an earthquake will not necessarily help a student learn about the respiratory system.

Task Analytic Sequencing. This sequencing strategy attempts to build on a learner's increasing store of prior knowledge. Prerequisite information is presented first, and then this information is built on in later instruction. This sequencing strategy also might be thought of as a *part-to-whole* strategy or *bottom-up* approach. This classic task analysis approach to curriculum sequencing generally is associated with behavioral views of learning and can be found in a wide variety of applications in special education as well as general education content. For example, in math, students would be taught simple addition and subtraction facts first, then use this information to solve two-step word problems later on.

Just-in-Time Sequencing. Topics are taught according to the order in which the students need them. Information that is needed soon is taught first. Information that is needed later is taught "just in time" for the learner to use it. For example, students might be taught to decode or sight-read a small set of high frequency words early in a beginning reading curriculum. Later on, less frequently encountered words would be taught as they occur in the reading material the students encounter.

Whole-to-Part Sequencing. This sequencing strategy presents general information first and then introduces more specific information. This strategy is more or less the opposite of the Task Analytic approach described above. For example, in a science class, students might first learn about general life systems, such as respiration and reproduction, and then learn about the parts and functions of plant and animal cells. In math, students might learn to develop their own approach to solving problems using manipulatives before they learn to do the specific computations involved. The Whole-to-Part sequencing strategy is closely associated with constructivist and cognitive views of learning.

Decisions About Time

In practice, curriculum and instruction usually involve a blending of sequencing strategies. For example, to teach beginning reading, an effective teacher may teach decoding as a prerequisite skill (Task Analytic approach), teach frequently occurring words as sight words (Just-In-Time approach), and employ a combination of written and oral language activities that enable students to gain a holistic view of what reading entails (Whole-to-Part approach).

It is important to consider the scope as well as short- and long-term goals of curriculum when deciding how to sequence information to ensure that students have an adequate opportunity to learn the things we want them to know by the time they need to know it. Teachers also must avoid curriculum omissions that will place a student at a disadvantage later on. However, it is critical that teachers not get stuck in the idea of "readiness" as they make decisions about time and curriculum. Many students who have learning problems require consistent, direct instruction and many trials to learn important basic skills such as reading and computation. These students may never have the opportunity to work toward the challenging outcomes contained in the curriculum frameworks if they are not deemed ready to move on until they have learned basic readiness skills. Teachers must consider the short- and long-term goals of curriculum along with the sequencing strategies to avoid the "ready means never" dilemma.

FINDING THE GENERAL EDUCATION CURRICULUM

The nature of curriculum is such that it is nearly impossible to identify the definitive general curriculum. What constitutes the general curriculum will depend on the perspective from which it is viewed, the outcomes that are expected, and the manner in which it is implemented in the classroom. However, there is a clear expectation in IDEA, as well as in federal and state policies associated with standards-based reform, that students who have disabilities will have meaningful access to the curriculum in which their nondisabled peers receive instruction. At the same time, the long-standing traditions of equal protection and provision of an appropriate IEP are still central to IDEA. These seemingly competing demands will require teachers to pursue a thoughtful and comprehensive analysis of the core curriculum elements discussed in this chapter.

Purpose, Domain, and Time

In this chapter, we have discussed these core elements of purpose, domain, and time as separate entities, but in reality, curriculum involves a complex interaction of these components. Therefore, the process of finding the general curriculum requires a multidimensional thinking strategy.

The process of sorting out the complex and dynamic mix of curriculum elements to find the general curriculum requires a "triage" mindset. The most pressing or urgent needs must be addressed first, and then secondary and tertiary curriculum goals are established. The goals of the general curriculum will be different for different individuals or groups. Special education generally is concerned with the needs of individual students, but planning for an individual student must take place within the larger context of the curriculum outcomes expected for all students. In Chapter 6, we will discuss the process of linking the larger context of curriculum to the specific needs of an individual student in the IEP process. We'll confine our discussion here to identifying what it is all students will be expected to learn.

The Present

Time is the overarching organizing structure within which the general curriculum is to be found. We view the curriculum through the continuously moving window of The Present to conduct a forward and backward looking analysis and decide how curricular time should be allocated. Specifically, we want to know *what should be taught* and *in what sequence it should be taught.* This is where the triage approach comes in. Of all the information that potentially could be included in the curriculum, what is the *most* important? Remember, be aware of seductive details and curriculum overload. Just because a publisher included some esoteric bit of information in a textbook does not mean you need to allocate valuable curriculum time to it.

For any particular student or group of students, these questions of what to teach and when to teach it require identification of the essential knowledge that will be needed in the future as well as the critical knowledge that has already been learned. Of course, these two pieces of information are linked, but the starting point for this analysis lies in the future.

Looking Ahead and Looking Back

The most important decision in finding the general curriculum is to identify the enduring knowledge that is at the core of the intended curriculum, standards, benchmarks, and indicators. As we discussed earlier in this chapter, the standards are anchored several years in the future. Objectives and benchmarks are narrower and will be accomplished sooner. However, curriculum standards are not isolated or arbitrary. Curriculum standards are situated in the larger context of the subject matter domains from which they are sampled. For example, a standard that requires students to "use geographic tools such as maps and charts to understand the spatial arrangement of people, places and resources on the Earth" has relevance beyond the simple task of locating specific places on a map during a test. Rather, the point of such a standard is for students to learn to "think like a geographer" (Harper, 1990) and to eventually have informed opinions about issues such as population growth, protection of endangered species, global warming, or geopolitics. In other words, the general curriculum is not just a set of goals contained in a set of guidelines established by the state. The general curriculum represents a meaningful sample of a much larger knowledge domain that extends far beyond the context of the classroom.

Identifying the enduring knowledge associated with the intended curriculum requires deep understanding of the disciplines. Educators who have only a superficial understanding of a particular subject matter domain associated with the intended curriculum will be unable to engage in this analysis and should seek the assistance of content specialists. Of course, few teachers are expected to have extensive expertise in more than a few domains, so finding the general curriculum almost certainly requires a collaborative process among thoughtful, knowledgeable teachers.

The desired outcome of this process is a set of concise statements delineating the most critical knowledge that all students will be expected to learn as a result of working in the curriculum and the approximate time frame in which the student would need to have acquired the knowledge. This list need not be exhaustive, but it should represent the most enduring, salient knowledge all students will need to learn. This knowledge then becomes the top priority in the curriculum triage.

A word of caution here though. Although we just said that some degree of content *expertise* is required in this process, be careful not to create a list of the knowledge and skills that would be required of a content *expert*. You are looking at the core and essential knowledge. Again, be careful to avoid curriculum overload. It is not necessary for everyone who studies history, mathematics, geography, or science in school to become a historian, mathematician, geographer, or scientist. The goal is to provide all students access to the information they will need to become effective members of society and to peruse a variety of postschool options. Further study in the disciplines is only one of those options.

When the enduring knowledge that all students must learn has been clarified, it is possible to start mapping backward from the future to the present to decide what will be needed in the future that has not been learned yet. This final step in finding the general curriculum entails looking back at previously taught curriculum as well as evaluation of the learned curriculum to decide how to allocate curriculum time in the present. At this point, it is important to consider any sequencing strategies that were used in previous taught curriculum, as well as the actual learned curriculum students bring with them to the present.

For groups of students, this analysis can focus on documents, curriculum materials, and teacher judgment. However, in the context of special education, it is likely that there will be concern with the prior knowledge and future needs of a particular student.

CONCLUSION

At the beginning of this chapter, we said that curriculum is at the center of standards-based reform because it is through curriculum that students are provided the opportunity to learn. As you think about ways to provide access to the general education curriculum for all students, it may be helpful to keep in mind some of the characteristics of curriculum that we discussed. Remember that the general education curriculum includes the full range of courses, activities, lessons, and materials used routinely by the general population of a school. Even though the intended curriculum is the official, or adopted, curriculum often contained in state or district policy, the learned curriculum is what really counts. This is what students actually learn as a result of being in the classroom and interacting with the intended and taught curriculum. Decisions about what to include or exclude from curriculum must take into account the variables of domain, time, and organization that underlie curriculum. But curriculum is only part of the picture. Ensuring access to the general education curriculum also requires attention to the way people learn and the strategies teachers can use to help all students become expert learners. That's what we'll discuss in the next chapter.

3 The Learning-Teaching Connection

One of the most direct results of the research on learning is that the notion of what it means to be a teacher has changed considerably in recent years. The focus in schools has shifted from drill and practice and rote learning to promoting students' understanding and use of subject matter content. Truly effective teachers are able to make crucial links between *curriculum* and *instruction* by attending to the way their students learn. However, being an effective teacher involves more than simply having a large toolbox of teaching techniques that are applied indiscriminately across content. Effective teachers have a deep understanding of their subject matter, know how people learn, understand theories of child development, possess a repertoire of research-validated teaching methods, and make effective use of standards-based curricula. Teachers who effectively orchestrate all of these variables are able to create opportunities for students to use, rather than simply acquire, information. Using information is the key to understanding.

Student understanding involves being able to perform in a variety of ways and contexts with a topic. Classrooms need to be learning environments in which performances of understanding are the norm and students are routinely expected to explain, provide evidence, find examples, generalize, apply concepts, create analogies, and represent information in novel ways.

This chapter presents an overview of findings from recent research on learning that can help all students access the general curriculum. We will examine some of the critical processes involved in learning and memory, and we will look at ways research has shown how teachers can enhance student learning by designing instruction that supports those processes.

LEARNING RESEARCH AND IMPLICATIONS FOR TEACHING

The new science of learning has been extremely influential in generating research into the ways humans learn and remember and is having a profound influence on both the curriculum and instruction (Bransford, Brown, & Cocking, 2000). Teachers must be able to design classroom learning environments that put into practice what the science of learning has revealed about how people learn. These classroom learning environments must be learner centered, knowledge centered, assessment centered, and community centered (see Box 3.1.).

Instruction that emphasizes these fundamental learning processes has been found to be particularly important for students who have learning problems. For example, students who have learning disabilities tend to make poor use of learning strategies such as rehearsal and planning, and they often have poor skills in remembering. However, there is considerable evidence that the performance of students who have learning problems can be improved when they are provided with supports for storing and retrieving information.

Box 3.1 Classroom Learning Environments

The National Research Council Commission on Behavioral and Social Sciences and Education published a highly influential report titled *How People Learn: Brain, Mind, Experience, and School* edited by John D. Bransford, Ann L. Brown, and Rodney R. Cocking (2000). This report summarizes the implications of the new science of learning for teachers and identifies four attributes of classroom learning environments that can optimize student learning:

1. In **learner-centered** learning environments, teachers are able to build on the conceptual and cultural knowledge that students bring to school with them. Teachers must pay close attention to students' skills, attitudes, and beliefs to find out what students think in the context of specific problems.
2. In **knowledge-centered** learning environments, teachers must pay direct attention to what is taught (information, subject matter), why it is taught (understanding), and how students will be expected to perform to demonstrate mastery.
3. In **assessment-centered** learning environments, teachers make skilled use of formative assessments to monitor student progress. Formative assessments permit the teacher to see students' preconceptions and thinking and then design instruction accordingly.
4. In **community-centered** learning environments, there are norms for the classroom and school, as well as connections to the outside world, that support core learning values. It is recognized that all learning is influenced by the context in which it takes place, and classrooms are viewed as communities that exist within school communities intricately connected to the larger communities of homes, businesses, and other structures within which students live and operate.

HELP STUDENTS DEVELOP MEANINGFUL PATTERNS OF INFORMATION

What is the difference between a "novice" and an "expert"?
What does it really mean to "understand" something?
Are some people better learners than others?

Recall and understanding are not simply the products of hours of drill or experience with a set of facts or skills. Rather, recall and understanding are related to how well a learner forms meaningful patterns of information in long-term memory. Both the structure of the underlying knowledge and experience a learner has had with similar information are important. If students have a sufficient base of information that is organized into meaningful patterns, they will be more likely to recognize and organize new or related knowledge about the same topic.

When something is stored in memory, it becomes part of a network in which various types of information (facts, propositions, concepts, and relationships) constitute "nodes." The more nodes and the more connections among nodes learners have, the better they will be at thinking, learning, recalling, and problem solving. Learners whose knowledge networks contain few connections among information or whose information is not well organized have a difficult time with learning and recall tasks. However, when a learner's knowledge network is well organized and includes many nodes that are well linked, learning, recalling, and problem solving can occur much more effectively. The key difference between novices and experts is that experts have elaborate, well-organized knowledge structures.

Try this. Think about the word "butterflies." What other words come to mind?

Perhaps you thought of types of butterflies, such as "Monarchs" or "Skippers." Maybe you thought of the life cycle of butterflies, and the words "chrysalis" or "pupa" came to mind. Maybe you conjured up words having to do with the features of butterflies, such as "wings," "camouflage" or "antennae." Perhaps you thought of all these ideas at the same time.

The terms that the word "butterflies" might prompt you to recall are all part of your knowledge network about "butterflies." Someone with expert knowledge of butterflies would be able to access an elaborate network that contained detailed information about butterfly life cycles, anatomy, subspecies, and habitats. Someone with novice butterfly knowledge might recall superficial information and few details. This difference is illustrated in Figures 3.1 and 3.2.

Figure 3.1 shows the pattern of information that a middle school student might develop during a unit about butterflies and moths. The network contains considerable background information, including attributes of butterflies and moths, examples of each, and some specialized vocabulary such as "chrysalis" and "metamorphosis." The information is organized more or less hierarchically, with meaningful connections among the various pieces of information and out to other information networks not directly pertaining to butterflies and moths. Generally, the information in the network is correct although some of it may be

Figure 3.1 Meaningful Pattern of Information About Butterflies and Moths

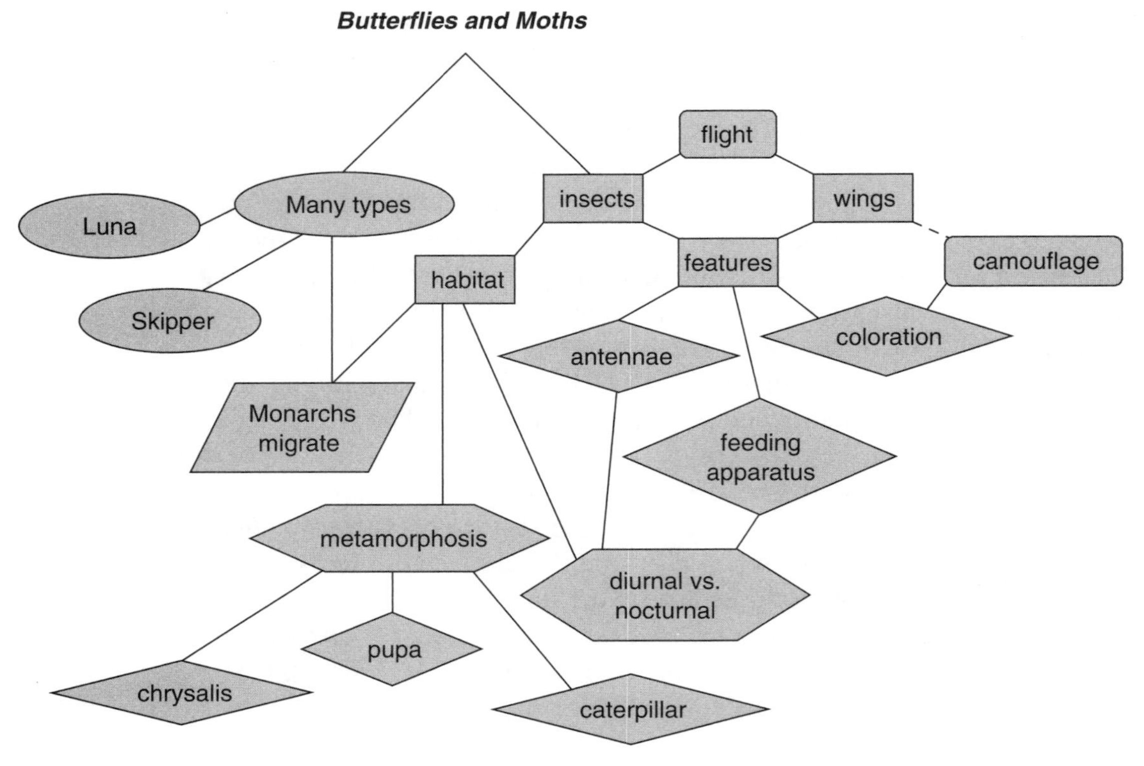

Figure 3.2 Novice Network of Information About Butterflies and Moths

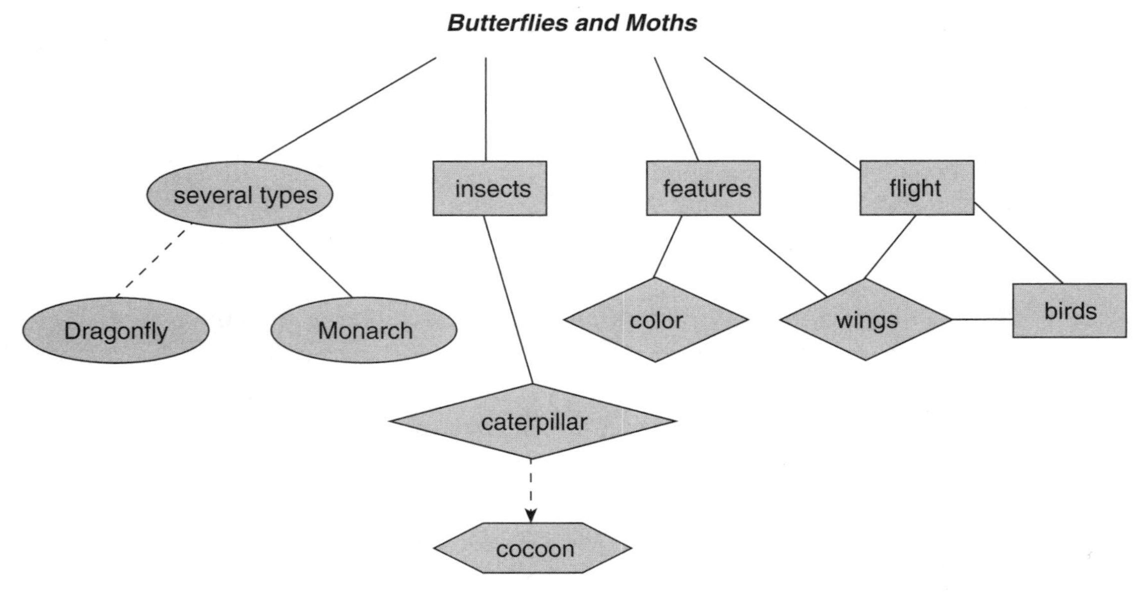

incomplete. For example, the student may be a little hazy on the relationship between coloration of butterfly and moth wings as a means of camouflage from predators, such as birds. The student also is not clear about processes that occur in different phases of the butterfly life cycle.

Figure 3.2 shows the network of a student who has only a minimal understanding of butterflies and moths. This figure might represent the network of a student who has not studied the butterfly unit. There is less information represented, and therefore, there are fewer connections. Also, the network contains some inaccurate information, such as the inclusion of dragonflies under the category of butterflies and moths, as well as a misconception about the butterfly life cycle. The most elaborated area of this student's information network pertains to the attribute of flight and the resemblance of butterflies to birds, which also fly. The good news is that this student is in control of some key information on which to build. For example, the student knows that there are several types of butterflies and moths and is able to name one example. The student also knows that butterflies are classified as insects. This is prior knowledge that a teacher can build on to help the student construct a more elaborate knowledge network.

The importance of the manner in which students organize information becomes clear during thinking and problem solving. Consider the thinking processes that the two students represented in Figures 3.1 and 3.2 might engage in when solving the problem presented in Box 3.2.

Solving the problem in Box 3.2 requires students to use information about the differences between moths and butterflies (antennae, body type, coloration, time of day when active) and the life cycles of butterflies and moths (unlikely to make holes in leaves as adults). The student with the well-organized pattern of information about butterflies and moths (Figure 3.1) would probably be better equipped to solve the problem and present a cogent rationale than the student whose knowledge structure is less well formed (Figure 3.2). The key to helping all students succeed in the general curriculum is to teach students to think like experts.

CREATING EXPERTS

Although experts do have more background knowledge and experience, the real advantage they have over novices is that they organize information in long-term memory more efficiently. Experts are able to analyze and remember larger chunks of information because they store information in categories rather than as separate bits of information. Experts also are able to process information faster than novices because they can search long-term memory more efficiently.

For example, when asked to solve problems, beginning physics students rely on formulas whereas experienced physics students or teachers quickly move to link the problem to certain principles or laws. Similarly, in a classic study that compared high school students to actual historians on a set of history problems, novice historian high school students actually remembered more dates than professional expert historians, but the experts were far superior in

Box 3.2 Keying-out Insect Samples Problem

Jenna's family has a plot in the community garden. Jenna noticed that there are holes in the edges of the leaves of some of the tomato plants, and she wants to try to figure out how the holes got there. She has seen several kinds of insects flying around and crawling on the plants, and she thinks they might have something to do with the problem. Jenna collects samples of three of the flying insects and now needs to key them out. Here is a description of each sample:

Sample 1

Collected at 11:00 a.m. near daisy plants.

- Wingspan is 6 cm; length 5 cm.
- Has four wings.
- Front and rear wings are not attached to one another.
- Wings are yellow with black spots, yellowish grey underneath.
- Body is slender, smooth, and light yellow.
- Mouth looks likes a long straw.
- Has six legs.
- A pair of antennae. Each antenna is black and has a small knob at the end.

Sample 2

Collected at 9:30 p.m. near streetlight.

- Wingspan is 4 cm; length 5 cm.
- Has four wings.
- Wings are grey with dark brown streaks.
- Front and rear wings are connected to one another.
- Body is thick, fuzzy, and grey.
- Mouth looks like a short straw.
- Has six legs.
- A pair of antennae. Each antenna is reddish brown and shaped like a comb.

Sample 3

Collected 4:00 p.m. near tomato plants.

- Wingspan is 2 cm; length 1.5 cm.
- Has four wings.
- Wings are clear with brown lines.
- Front and rear wings are not attached to one another.
- Body is thick, fuzzy, and is yellow with black stripes.
- Has six legs. Rear legs are thick at top and fuzzy.
- Mouth looks like pliers.
- Antennae are smooth, straight, and black.

Here is what you need to do:

1. Use what you have learned about butterflies and moths to help Jenna figure out what she has collected. Tell whether each sample is a butterfly, a moth, or something else.
2. Do you think any of the samples Jenna has collected are making the holes in her tomato plants? Write a short paragraph that explains your answer.

elaborating and explaining certain events and in using different approaches to thinking about the problem (Wineburg, 1991).

All students can develop patterns of information that will allow them to perform more like experts. In the rest of this chapter, we will discuss things teachers can do to help their students learn, remember, and use information in the general curriculum like experts.

TEACH TO IMPROVE YOUR STUDENTS' MEMORIES

All information is not the same. People learn and remember different types of information differently, and instruction must be matched to the type of information to be learned. Because facts must be memorized, instruction should provide ample opportunities for recall and practice. Concepts require instruction that focuses on critical features and exemplars. Principles and processes often are best taught as "if-then" relationships. For example, rote memorization of the names of the stages of butterfly metamorphosis (egg, caterpillar, pupa, chrysalis, butterfly) in preparation for recall on a vocabulary test won't necessarily help students remember the order in which the stages occur, nor will it help them to recognize a chrysalis if they find one attached to a leaf on a mild weed plant. On their own, facts are hard to remember and are quickly forgotten unless they are part of a meaningful network of information.

Teachers can help their students learn and remember like experts when they are clear about the types of information they want their students to learn (facts, concepts, rules, procedures, strategies, etc.) and make clear the manner in which the information will be used. The idea is to match your choice of instructional strategies with the type of information you are asking your students to learn. The format of the information you want to teach determines your choice of instructional strategy. The key elements of instruction for teaching each type of information are summarized in Figure 3.3.

The structures and organization of information in long-term memory also govern how efficiently students use their knowledge and acquire new information. If information is poorly organized in memory, it is more difficult for students to activate relevant knowledge and connect it with new information. If no meaning can be attached to the new information, it may fade from memory, or it may be "misclassified," leading to development of misunderstanding or mistakes. For example, suppose a student memorizes a set of disconnected facts about the U.S. states (e.g., there are 50 states, each has a capital, some were the original 13 colonies). Later, when presented with new examples of government structures associated with the United States (e.g., District of Columbia, Puerto Rico, or Guam) the student develops the misconception that they must be separate countries because they are not on the list of U.S. states memorized earlier.

Learning and remembering are easier when information is presented in a meaningful context rather than as disparate bits of information. When teachers are mindful about the reason for asking students to learn something, they are better prepared to help the students develop well-organized patterns of information. But being mindful takes some thinking and planning ahead of

Figure 3.3 Instruction to Teach Various Types of Information

Information Type	*Cognitive Tasks Performed by Learner*	*Implications for Teaching*
Facts	• Move information from working memory to long-term memory • Recall information on demand • Link new information with prior knowledge	• Organize information prior to teaching through use of chunking • Build in sufficient practice • Build elaboration into later instructional sequences
Concepts	• Discriminate examples from nonexamples of concept class • Generate new examples not previously encountered	• Carefully select examples and nonexamples • Juxtapose examples to focus on salient features • Use a model-lead-practice format for instruction
Rules	• Discern multiple parts of the rule relationship • Predict outcomes from part of rule • Discriminate occasions when rule applies	• Teach each part of the rule • Show relationship among rule parts • Incorporate expanded examples into later instructional sequences
Strategies	• Recall component parts of strategy • Recognize occasions when strategy is useful • Initiate strategy when needed • Evaluate use of strategy through self monitoring	• Teach each of the component parts of the strategy • Model strategy and lead learner through use • Show occasions when strategy is useful

time. Here are some questions to ask yourself as you are planning instruction for your students:

- What type of information am I asking my students to learn?
- Why do I want my students to remember this information?
- How is this information connected to other things they already know?
- How is this information related to what it is the students will need to learn in the future?
- How will the students use this information?
- When will my students need to use this information?
- What is the most efficient way for students to learn this information?

HELP STUDENTS ATTEND TO WHAT YOU WANT THEM TO LEARN

As information from the environment is detected through one of the senses, it is held briefly until it can be analyzed. This analysis involves matching the incoming stimulus with a recognizable pattern already stored in memory. To allocate attention to something, a student must select it from among many competing stimuli that occur simultaneously. These stimuli can include the obvious, such as other students talking, noise outside the room, or materials students have at their desks. Less obvious but equally distracting competing stimuli could include information on bulletin boards or walls, extra sidebar or enhancement features contained in curriculum materials, or poorly worded teacher instructions. Teachers can assist students in this process by limiting the amount of information to which they ask students to attend at any one time. For example, teachers who use clear, concise wording in their presentations often are better able to maintain and focus student attention than those who require their students to pick the most important information out of an endless stream of superfluous "happy talk." The idea is to say less but make every word count. Which of the following teachers do you think will be more successful at helping students attend to important information in a middle school math class?

Mr. Albertson: [*standing in front of room*] Yeah. You guys are a bunch of math monsters. You got the goal and extra points. Yeah, OK now when you're done with the worksheet, just put it in the basket, OK? And then you can go ahead and start working on the homework. But first, you need to finish up the challenge problem, right? But hey! Remember it's not the same as the one we had yesterday, but it kind of looks the same. It's tricky, uh huh. It's a tricky one all right. Kind of a faker-outer. OK, now your homework starts on page 78. Just do the odd-numbered problems. You can work together at your table, but you need to do your own work. If you're finished with the challenge problem, just put it aside, and we'll talk about it in a little while. Go ahead and start working. [*Begins writing homework assignment on the board*].

Mr. Harlan: Who is finished with the worksheet? Raise your hands. Keep them up. The rest of you, meet me at the back table. That's Jana, Anthony, James, and Karissa. Bring your worksheet with you. Everyone else, put your hands down now. Take out your math book. Your homework assignment is on the board right here [*points, reads the assignment aloud*]. OK. What page is the homework on? Everyone. [*Students respond chorally*] You may begin working on the homework now. No talking, please. [*Moves to back table, checking to see that students are on correct page along the way. Works with small group on the worksheet. Five minutes later, they return to their seats*]. OK, everyone. Let's look at the challenge problem from this morning. Everyone take it out and put it on your desk in front of you while we talk about it. It's the yellow sheet of paper. [*Walks around the room to check on whether all students have the challenge problem out*]. Listen. What is an "unknown"? Raise your hand if you remember. Yes, thank you Cesar, an unknown is the variable we need to find when we solve a problem. At your table group, decide: What are the unknowns in the challenge problem? Table recorders raise your hands. OK, you people be sure to write down the variables your group identifies.

Humans have an extremely limited capacity to attend to information coming in from the environment. Visual information begins to fade after only one half of a second, and auditory stimuli are held for only about 3 seconds. Information that isn't attended to or recognized fades away quickly and is replaced by new incoming information. Effective teachers recognize this problem and use a variety of strategies to focus and maintain student attention and aid in recognition. For example, Mr. Harlan uses directions that are short and specific. He asks students to respond frequently either physically (raise hands) or verbally. He manages large and small groups effectively so that all students get the support they need. He uses materials that make it easier to monitor student attention (i.e., the challenge problem presented on a yellow sheet of paper). He moves around the room frequently, and he makes effective use of seating arrangements and cooperative learning strategies.

Box 3.3 shows some classroom strategies that can promote attention and recognition. How many of these strategies can you find in Mr. Harlan's teaching?

Box 3.3 Classroom Strategies to Improve Attention and Recognition

- **Establish and keep schedules of classroom activities and events, and provide systematic reminders for students of the sequence in which activities will occur.** For example, post the daily schedule on the blackboard, and then periodically remind students to consult the schedule to see what is coming up next. This strategy cuts down on transition time and helps students focus their attention more quickly after a transition has been made.
- **Use a consistent set of signals to cue student attention.** Signals used with younger children can include bells, hand claps, verbal cues (e.g., "Eyes on me"), or turning the lights on and off. Older students may be cued with more subtle but consistent signals such as standing in front of the class to begin each new activity, turning the overhead projector on, or using age-appropriate verbal cues (e.g., "OK, now listen up").
- **Use clear, concise directions that focus on only one task at a time.** For example, use short specific directions such as, "Turn to page 73." Wait until everyone has turned to the correct page and then say, "Everyone, look at the problems on the bottom of page 73." Pause and then say, "Do the problems on the bottom of page 73. Show your work." This is better than giving complex, multistep directions such as, "Do the problems at the bottom of page 73 and be sure to show your work. Then, when you have finished those, you may work on the challenge problem on the board or else finish your journal writing from before."
- **Plan tasks according to the amount of attention required to complete them.** If a task is too long or requires students to attend to too many variables, their attention may drift. Break up lessons into smaller segments with different but related activities that require a variety of responses. For example, a math problem-solving lesson might

(Continued)

Box 3.3 (Continued)

start with a large group presentation and modeling, followed by a partner task using manipulatives, followed by a task students complete individually at their desk, followed by a group presentation and questioning to wrap up the lesson. Depending on the age of the students, each segment might last from 8 to 10 minutes. Of course, the transitions between lesson segments would need to be cued, as we discussed above, so that the students are told what they should be doing and to which aspects of the task they should be attending.

- **Use a variety of types of questions to aid recognition.** Students' attention wavers quickly if they are not challenged by teacher questioning or if the questions are too difficult. Ask a variety of related questions that require students to recall declarative information, make inferences, form opinions, and make evaluations. Also, avoid guessing games. Only ask questions that you think your students know how to answer.
- **Present information in more than one format.** This strategy assists students in attending to and recognizing salient information in instruction by focusing their attention on what is similar in the two formats (Case, 1985). Examples of this strategy include use of manipulatives to model math concepts, laboratory demonstrations to illustrate chemistry or physics problems, step-by-step illustrated descriptions of math problem solving, and teacher think-alouds paired with a demonstration of how to write a compare-contrast paragraph.
- **Employ brisk lesson pacing, and provide frequent opportunities for students to respond.** Choral responding can be used even with older students when it is embedded in age-appropriate and respectful contexts. Similarly, students can write responses on small whiteboards with erasable pens and then quickly hold them up during group lessons.
- **Frequently check to be sure your students are attending and understand your expectations.** Ask questions that require students to demonstrate understanding and attention rather than yes/no questions. For example, ask, "Bonnie, on what page are we all going to be working?" rather than "Bonnie, are you on the correct page?"

MAKE EFFECTIVE USE OF PRACTICE

Information that has been learned effectively is more likely to be remembered than information that is not integrated into a meaningful network. Naturally, the more often information is encountered, the more likely it will be easily retrieved when needed. However, it is important for teachers to employ the kind of practice that provides opportunities for students to use recently learned information. For example, practice sessions can be either *massed* or *distributed.*

Massed practice involves longer sessions of intense practice at irregular intervals. Cramming on the night before a test is an example of massed practice. Distributed practice refers to regularly scheduled practice sessions that may be shorter and less intense than massed practice. In general, distributed practice is much more effective than massed practice because it increases the frequency with which a learner encounters the to-be-learned information and activates relevant prior knowledge in long-term memory. Teachers can facilitate this process by systematically building in short practice sessions throughout the day and over subsequent days following introduction of new information.

Distributed practice also is important for building automaticity and fluency. Being fluent does not always mean being fast. It does, however, mean that the learner does not have to focus concentrated attention on trying to remember what to do. Fluency increases as a learner gains more experience with a task. For example, beginning readers must struggle with the decoding of every word because they have not learned letter-sound associations that fluent readers make automatically. Fluency is important because a person can only consciously attend a finite amount of information at any one time. A child who is struggling with basic word recognition cannot attend to all of the nuances of a paragraph or concepts and principles being presented.

MAKE EFFECTIVE USE OF SCAFFOLDING

Learning new information involves locating and activating information stored in knowledge networks and connecting the new thing to be learned with the information already in the knowledge network. When the learner does not have relevant prior knowledge to which the new information can be connected, the new information will seem meaningless and therefore will not be remembered.

When a student lacks sufficient prior knowledge to make a connection with new information being taught, the teacher must provide temporary supports, often called *scaffolding,* to augment the student's existing knowledge. Once the student has enough relevant information stored in long-term memory, the scaffolding can be removed. Scaffolding is a way of systematically transferring control of the skill or knowledge from the teacher to the student. Here are some things teachers can do to scaffold student learning:

1. Organize the information you want your students to learn before you teach it. Use advance organizers and graphic displays to show the structure of the information to be learned. When information can be organized into categories, show the superordinate and subordinate relationships among various elements of what you want your students to learn. When factual information can be chunked into meaningful clusters, make the chunking scheme explicit for students during instruction, rather than relying on them to make the links on their own. Instruction should begin with easy tasks and progress to more complex tasks as the learner develops more relevant and elaborate background knowledge.

2. Reduce the number of steps required to solve a problem. When you simplify the task, students can manage the various components of the problem-solving process. Once they have control of the smaller steps, they can begin to fit the steps together. After students have successfully solved simplified problems, they'll be ready to take on more complex versions of the task and apply similar problem-solving strategies. Introduce only a manageable amount of information. It is far better to break up large, complex problems into smaller segments and teach them over multiple lessons rather than try to teach everything at once. One of the most important skills in teaching is knowing how much to teach and at what pace to teach it.

3. Multiple skills or pieces of information that are likely to be confused should be separated. Introduce one, and delay introducing the second until the learner is firm on the first. If you doubt the importance of this guideline, think about how often young children confuse "left" and "right" when they have been taught the two concepts at the same time in a "This is my left hand; this is my right hand" format.

4. Provide direct assistance to help students activate prior knowledge already stored in long-term memory. Many teachers use a variety of techniques designed to stimulate recall, such as strategic questioning and recall diagrams. Never assume that students have fully learned what you may think they have learned or that they will be able to recall that information when they need it. You can facilitate recall directly by explicitly telling students what you want them to think about prior to presenting the new information. For example, use statements such as this to prompt recall:

Ms. D'Angelo: Yesterday, we learned that zero is the identity function in addition. Think about what happens when you *add* zero to a number. It stays the same. Today, we will learn about the identity function in multiplication. What do you think will happen when we *multiply* a number by the identity function?

5. Provide effective models of the performance you want the students to learn. When students lack prior knowledge, they may not know what correct use of the information looks like. For example, we would not expect someone to learn how to play a musical instrument if they had never heard someone else play it. Yet, teachers frequently ask their students to perform new, complex tasks with few, if any, models of correct performance. When students can see the steps they need to follow, they can match their own performance to the ideal version and monitor their own thinking during the learning process. Your instruction should provide multiple examples of the target skill or information. These examples should be sequenced and juxtaposed, so that the student can focus on the most salient features of what it is to be learned.

6. Mark the critical features of discrepancies between the students' performance and the "correct" performance. When your feedback to students is specific and focuses directly on errors or misconceptions, the students can zero in on that aspect of the task. Global "atta-boy" feedback provides little support for the learning process.

7. Incorporate elaboration tactics into your instruction. These tactics prompt students to think about new and previously learned information at the same time. Prompt students to paraphrase or summarize what they have learned in their own words. Provide students with structured study guides or note-taking supports that prompt simultaneous attention to old and new information. For example, students learning how to compute the area of a square might be prompted on a study guide to tell how the computation of area is similar to the computation of perimeter (assuming computation of perimeter is prior knowledge).

8. Provide adequate opportunities for guided practice before a student is required to use a skill or information independently. During guided practice, the learner uses the skill or information under close supervision, and the teacher provides immediate feedback to correct errors and support correct performance. Generally, students should be about 80% accurate under guided practice before they are required to perform independently.

HELP STUDENTS MANAGE THEIR OWN LEARNING

Expert learners are able to consciously regulate their thinking processes, behaviors, and performance while they learn. They are able to break tasks into manageable steps, organize time to plan ahead, and explain to themselves how to move through a task. Learners who are good at regulating their own learning can handle a greater quantity of information and more complex forms of information. Less skilled learners have less well-developed learning management systems, so they may have more information traffic jams and pile-ups, and information gets lost more often.

Managing one's own learning is not automatic but must be done intentionally and consciously. This function often is referred to as *metacognition* or *self-regulation* and generally involves the use of learned strategies. Self-regulation requires a learner to (a) be aware of what strategies or resources a learning task requires, (b) know how and when to use those strategies, and (c) be motivated to use the strategies. A number of specific strategies intended to help students regulate their own learning have been described in the literature in recent years, and a full description of them is beyond the scope of this chapter. However, most strategies fall into one of the following major categories: rehearsal, elaboration, organization, comprehension monitoring, or affect.

Rehearsal

Rehearsal strategies help students attend to information to be learned and then actively transfer that information to memory. Rehearsal strategies for learning simple information (e.g., facts such as dates, or simple concepts such as shapes or colors) generally involve active repetition of information presented during instruction. Rehearsal strategies for learning more complex information (e.g., expository material presented in a social studies textbook) can include repeating the material aloud, copying the material, taking detailed notes, and underlining important passages.

Students often need to be taught both how and when to use rehearsal strategies. Children in the primary grades do not spontaneously use rehearsal, even for learning basic information. Teachers of children at these grades should model simple rehearsal strategies and then explicitly instruct students to use them at appropriate times. By fifth grade, students may spontaneously use some rehearsal but often do not possess sufficient background knowledge to do so effectively. For example, they may not be able to accurately discriminate the most important information in a textbook passage or in an interactive lesson. Teachers can support students' use of rehearsal strategies to learn more complex information by explicitly instructing them to use the strategy, providing structured note-taking guides, and modeling specific strategies such as repeating important information aloud at the end of a passage.

Elaboration

Elaboration strategies help students make connections between new information to be learned and existing prior knowledge. When the student is able to see how the old and new information are related, the connection between them is strengthened. Elaboration helps students fill in the gaps.

When learning simple information such as labels and names or lists of facts, students could write or say sentences that would make the simple fact more meaningful. For example, students learning the name of the original 13 U.S. colonies might write or orally present sentences that tell the origins of each colony name. Elaboration strategies for learning more complex information can include creating analogies and metaphors, using imagery, answering multilevel questions (e.g., literal and inferential), and note taking. Note-taking and study guides can be constructed that teach students to distinguish between superordinate and subordinate information and paraphrase or summarize information in their own words. Mnemonics also is a commonly used and effective elaboration strategy. Again, because students do not spontaneously generate and use these strategies, teachers often must provide explicit instruction about how and when to use them.

Organization

Organizational strategies are aimed at helping students structure the information to be learned and then connect it to relevant prior knowledge. Clustering or *chunking* of information into categories is the most common organizing strategy for learning simple information. Although most skilled learners do this almost automatically, younger students or students who have learning problems often need to be taught how and when to use this strategy. Teachers can scaffold organizational strategies by arranging information into logical categories prior to instruction, by modeling and leading students through a process of categorizing information, and by pointing out patterns that may exist in the to-be-learned information. Other common strategies for organizing information include graphic organizers, chapter outlines, and expository summaries that show relationships among the pieces of information to be learned. For example, students might summarize cause-effect, chronological, or problem-solution patterns in textbook passages. Teachers can facilitate students' use of organizational strategies by modeling and leading students through use of outline techniques, by providing outlining worksheets in various forms of completion, or by providing blank graphic organizers as prereading study aids.

Comprehension Monitoring

Comprehension monitoring strategies help students use active and ongoing self-checking to determine how well information is being understood and connected with prior knowledge. Comprehension monitoring involves identifying goals for learning (particularly reading) and evaluating the degree to which those goals are being met. Some common and effective monitoring strategies include self-questioning, rereading, paraphrasing, and checking for inconsistencies. Teachers can scaffold students' use of comprehension monitoring strategies by modeling the process in think-aloud lessons and by breaking reading tasks into smaller segments and then periodically guiding the students to ask questions about the reading. Use of pre-during-post reading guides such as K-W-L questions (What Do I **K**now? What Do I **W**ant to Learn? What Did I **L**earn?) also aid comprehension monitoring.

Affect

Affective strategies are aimed at helping students approach learning tasks in a relaxed, positive state of mind and be effective during studying and learning activities. Common affective strategies include goal setting and time management activities, reducing external distractions by establishing a common time and place for studying, and using self-verbalizations to overcome negative attributions or expectations about learning.

TEACH FOR TRANSFER AND GENERALIZATION

How students learn new material greatly influences their ability to transfer that knowledge to other settings. Learning that involves understanding, as opposed to rote memorization of facts or procedures, is more likely to transfer to other situations or problems. However, a person could demonstrate complete understanding in one context and incomplete understanding in another. Therefore, one of the most important considerations in helping students transfer learning from one context to another is awareness of the kind of transfer expected.

One distinction commonly made is between *near* and *far* transfer. In a near transfer task, there is much overlap between the situation in which a skill is learned and the situation in which it is later used. An end-of-the-week test in multiplication that presents problems in exactly the same format in which they were learned would be an example of a near transfer task. Far transfer is required when there is little overlap between the original learning situation and the context in which the skill is required. Using the Pythagorean theorem to plan a skateboard park after learning to solve geometry problems in the classroom would be an example of a far transfer task.

It is also important to understand that prior knowledge can get in the way of new learning. For example, irregularities in basic letter-sound relationships can cause a beginning reader many difficulties in initial decoding, or when learning Spanish, a student might employ familiar English pronunciations. Teachers can detect and correct some of the more common ways in which a student can be tripped up by prior knowledge through use of questioning that requires students to explain why they solved a problem a certain way or gave a specific answer.

Transfer does not occur automatically, but teachers can support it. Box 3.4 shows some classroom strategies aimed at increasing transfer.

Box 3.4 Classroom Strategies to Improve Transfer

- **Provide opportunities for students to practice skills and apply knowledge in a variety of contexts.** It is important to help students build links in long-term memory that help them perceive similarities between various situations that would trigger use of a particular piece of information or procedure.
- **Systematically vary types of examples** from near to far **transfer.** Gradually introduce elements of the transfer situation into the examples students encounter so that the transition from the learned task to the transfer task takes the form of many small near transfer steps rather than a single far transfer leap. You can vary the size of the steps according to both the amount of prior knowledge your students can readily activate and the distance of the transfer task from the original learning task. For example, to help students transfer subtraction of three-digit numerals in columnar problems to a two-step word problem involving money, you might systematically introduce the following elements in successive lessons or examples: addition and subtraction problems involving decimals, addition and subtraction involving money labels, one-step word problems involving two-digit and three-digit subtraction, two-step word problems involving subtraction with decimals, and finally two-step word problems involving two-digit subtraction with money labels.
- **Model strategies that show how previously learned information can be used in a new situation.** Teachers can use think-aloud procedures or other ways to make covert thought processes observable by students. For example, while demonstrating how to conduct an Internet

(Continued)

Box 3.4 (Continued)

or library search, a teacher might model a set of problem-solving self-questions taught during a math class, for example, What is my goal? What do I know already? What do I need to find out? What steps do I need to follow to reach my goal? Have I reached my goal yet?

- **Provide cues in situations where students are required to transfer previously learned information**. For example, you might prompt students' use of a prewriting strategy learned in the context of narrative story writing when they are writing a letter with a statement such as this one: "You can plan your letter using brainstorming the same way you did when you made up the stories we wrote last week. Who remembers how to use brainstorming?"

THE LEARNING-TEACHING CONNECTION

Instruction must be designed on the basis of what it is students will be expected to learn. The nature of the information shapes the instruction. However, humans use different cognitive processes to learn different types of information, so it is only through careful consideration of both the information and the thinking processes required for learning that information that an effective learning-teaching connection can be made. Here is a checklist of questions to ask yourself about the instruction you provide in your classroom. As you look at the checklist, think about ways you can improve the learning-teaching connections for your students.

✓ **What strategies do you use to focus your students' attention and aid their recognition of "important-to-remember information"?**

• As a stimulus (or *information*) from the environment is detected through one of the senses, it is held briefly in *sensory memory* until it can be analyzed. The primary functions here are attention and recognition. Effective teachers use a variety of strategies to focus and maintain student attention and aid in recognition. These strategies include use of signals to indicate the beginning and end of activities; movement, gestures, and speech patterns that maintain attention; variation in materials and activities; and use of a variety of types of questions to aid recognition.

✓ **What strategies do you use to provide opportunities for practice in your classroom?**

• The more often information is encountered, the more likely it is to be easily retrieved when needed. This is why it is important for teachers to provide opportunities for their students to practice using recently learned information. Distributed practice is much more effective than massed practice because it increases the frequency with which a learner encounters the to-be-learned information and activates relevant prior knowledge in long-term memory.

✓ **What scaffolding strategies do you employ in your teaching?**

• When a student lacks sufficient prior knowledge to make a connection with new information being taught, the teacher must provide temporary supports, often called scaffolding, to augment the student's existing knowledge.

✓ **How do you help your students organize information as they learn it?**

• Learners develop structures and schemes for organizing information memory. These structures govern comprehension as well as how efficiently learners use what they already know. Learning failure can occur if the learner's long-term memory is poorly organized.

✓ **What strategies do you use to help your students activate prior knowledge?**

• Learners who have a large, well-organized, readily accessible store of prior knowledge are better able to process information through working memory than those who lack prior knowledge or are less able to access information stored in long-term memory.

✓ **How do you facilitate transfer and generalization?**

• How a student learns new material greatly influences the ability to transfer that knowledge to other settings. A person could demonstrate complete understanding in one context and incomplete understanding in another. Therefore, it is important to provide opportunities for students to practice skills and apply knowledge in a variety of contexts and to discriminate the characteristics of different situations that require information learned previously in a different context.

4 Assessment That Supports Access to the General Education Curriculum

Special educators sometimes seem to have a preoccupation with assessment and evaluation. The roots of this tradition probably can be found in the medical model that dominated special education until very recently. In 1975, when the original special education legislation, Public Law (PL) 94–142, was passed, the prevailing general education curriculum and instructional programs in a student's school were viewed as variables largely extraneous to a child's disability. It was thought that, for a student with disabilities to benefit from a free and *appropriate* public education, a school needed to match the correct intervention with the student's unique characteristics, identified through individually administered diagnostic tests of the student's abilities. In this diagnosis-treatment model, a student was tested, learning strengths and deficits were identified, and individual goals, objectives, and strategies were devised to ameliorate the deficits. Assessments and interventions focused on immediate and discrete skill deficits and frequently were conducted in isolation from the larger general education curriculum.

As a result, Individualized Education Programs (IEPs) often were a collection of isolated skill objectives that led to isolated instructional interventions provided in a special classroom or setting. The student's program may have been individualized, but it also often was separated from the larger scope and sequence of an organized curriculum. Indeed, the IEP *was* the curriculum for many students. This traditional diagnosis-treatment model of special education often resulted in educational goals that were isolated from or had little connection to the general curriculum goals.

The original federal special education law has been reauthorized, revised, renumbered, and renamed several times in the past 30 years. With the most recent reauthorization in November 2004, the law became PL 108–446, the Individuals with Disabilities Education Improvement Act, still referred to as IDEA. As a result of these revisions, special education has changed drastically.

The focus has shifted from a concern with remediation of developmental deficits to an emphasis on preparation of students with disabilities for postschool environments through access to the general education curriculum (Browder et al., in press).

In this book, we have been talking about a model of special education in which a student's IEP focuses on the accommodations, services, and support needed to help the student progress in the general curriculum. This new conception of special education first was communicated in the 1997 IDEA amendments and is reinforced in the No Child Left Behind Act (NCLB) as well as in the most recent reauthorization of IDEA. These laws clearly emphasize the principle that the education of students with disabilities must be anchored in a general education curriculum and must be based on content and achievement standards.

The IEP is neither a substitute for the general education curriculum nor a random collection of objectives but rather a tool for implementing a standards-driven curriculum. Further, students do not access the general curriculum simply because they are placed in general education classrooms or because they receive instruction based on general education curricular materials. The assumption communicated in IDEA and NCLB is that each student will be instructed in the same subject matter defined by a state's content standards.

For students to progress in the general curriculum, educators are required to use a new set of assessment and measurement tools and to think differently about the role of assessment in instruction. Assessment must be aimed at providing evidence to help IEP teams decide which curricular and instructional accommodations, modifications, or both are needed for a student with disabilities to make adequate progress in the general curriculum. In Chapter 6, we discuss a decision-making process that can guide IEP teams. In this chapter, we will explore assessment strategies that underlie this decision-making process.

ASSESSMENT AND DECISION MAKING

All educational assessment is aimed at answering questions. Sometimes, the question is as straightforward as "Is this student ready to move on to the next level of the reading curriculum?" or "Have my students learned the most important concepts related to electromagnetism?" At other times, the question is much more complex, such as "Does this student have a learning disability?" or "Is this an effective school?" However, the ultimate purpose of any educational assessment system should be to support valid inferences about student performance and progress.

The assessment process used for development of an IEP must generate multiple forms of evidence of the student's present level of academic achievement and functional performance. This body of evidence should consist primarily of classroom-based and other authentic performance measures rather than formal tests, although IDEA does require consideration of state and local assessments. Minimally, a team will want to collect multiple samples of the student's performance in a variety of relevant and meaningful contexts. For example, before developing an IEP goal in the area of "written expression," various samples of writing, such as completed worksheets, journal entries, letters, and stories, might be collected. These samples could be collected during classes where written expression is taught, as well as in other classes, such as social studies, math, and science, where writing skills are used. It may also be useful to collect evidence of the student's written expression in nonschool applications, such as at home or in recreational settings.

There is no single best process for developing an IEP. Similarly, there is no standard assessment battery that would facilitate development of an IEP. Each student and each context may require a unique combination of assessment information in order for the IEP team to make valid planning and instructional decisions. In general, the assessment process necessary for creating an IEP includes the following major tasks:

- Determination of the student's present level of academic achievement and functional performance in the general education curriculum
- Specification of goals and objectives or benchmarks
- Identification of accommodations and modifications that will enable the student to access the general curriculum
- Monitoring of the student's progress in the general curriculum to evaluate the effectiveness of the plan

Decisions about how the student will participate in district and state large-scale assessment programs and the settings in which the student will receive educational services follow from these major planning tasks and occur after goals, objectives, and educational supports have been identified.

There are four general assessment questions that can guide this planning process:

- What will typical students be expected to do (in, e.g., math, science, and reading) during the time frame addressed by the IEP (a grading period, semester, or year)? This question requires the multidisciplinary team to clearly identify the content standards from the general education curriculum that will be addressed as well as the level of achievement expected of the typical student.

- What is the student's present level of academic achievement and functional performance in the general education curriculum? This question requires collection of various types of evidence regarding the student's performance in specific content domains as well as input from parents, teachers, and other team members. To answer this question, the team needs to directly observe and assess the student's performance on standards-based tasks and make a judgment about the student's current proficiency in performing those tasks.

- In what ways does the student's disability affect his or her involvement and progress in the general education curriculum? In addition to specific skill deficits such as in reading or math, the team needs to consider such things as attention, organization, and other learning processes. This fine-grained analysis of the direct impact of the student's disability on performance is necessary for determination of the accommodations, modifications, or both that will enable the student to progress in the general education curriculum.

- Is the student making progress in the general education curriculum? The IEP team must describe how each student's progress toward their annual IEP goals will be measured as well as when and how periodic progress reports will be provided. This question requires the team to think about various reference standards with which to compare the student's performance. The team must decide if the student's current level of performance represents improved proficiency over previous performance. This decision will have a direct influence on the types of special education services provided and the settings in which they are provided.

WHAT WILL TYPICAL STUDENTS BE EXPECTED TO DO DURING THE TIME FRAME ADDRESSED BY THE IEP?

As we discussed in the last chapter, the general education curriculum in today's schools is built around state content standards. On their own, the content and achievement standards do not constitute the curriculum, but they do provide a common vocabulary for the IEP team to use as it considers what performance is expected in the general education curriculum. Standards define what *all* students are expected to demonstrate as a result of instruction in the general curriculum. Without a clear understanding of those expectations, the IEP team will be unable to define for a particular student what access to, and progress in, the curriculum means. As we discussed in Chapter 2, a focus on standards requires consideration of the critical, enduring knowledge associated with the general education curriculum.

The difficulty that IEP planning teams face is that the IEP goals must reflect annual learning targets that will enable the student to eventually demonstrate proficiency with respect to the broader and longer term standards. To address this dilemma, the IEP team must attend to the three important attributes of curriculum discussed in Chapter 2: immediacy, specificity, and sequencing. Focus on these three dimensions of the general curriculum will help the team determine how soon, or in which contexts, typical students are expected to demonstrate performance; the level of detail or focus communicated in the standards; and the order in which information is to be learned and performed.

Once these expectations for typical students are clearly identified, it is possible to analyze the performance of the specific student for whom an IEP is to be written. The content and achievement standards established for a student's grade-level peers usually represent the starting point for the IEP decisions that follow. It is true that a very small portion of the population of students with disabilities may be held to alternate achievement standards and assessed differently, but under NCLB, these are to be based on the prevailing general education standards.

WHAT IS THE STUDENT'S PRESENT LEVEL OF ACADEMIC ACHIEVEMENT AND FUNCTIONAL PERFORMANCE IN THE GENERAL EDUCATION CURRICULUM?

Establishing a student's present level of academic achievement and functional performance in the general education curriculum requires the use of direct measures of the thinking and problem solving associated with the content in the general curriculum. The distinction between *direct* and *indirect* assessment is an important one when we consider the kind of thinking and problem solving implied by the content standards and curriculum frameworks found in most schools. Direct measures are those that allow observation of the thinking or problem solving a student is expected to learn. Indirect measures are those that require the teacher to make an inference about the student's ability to use the thinking or problem solving process they are expected to have learned.

Direct measures generally require students to solve problems using evaluation, prediction, and application of concepts and principles. Indirect measures are those that simply require students to summarize and reiterate facts, concepts, and principles but never use them to solve complex problems. The example from science in Box 4.1 illustrates this distinction.

Box 4.1 Examples of Direct and Indirect Measures

One of the benchmarks for a science standard in a particular state curriculum framework is that students will understand how interactions among systems can cause changes in matter and energy. An indicator for this benchmark is that students will be able to explain how human use of natural resources affects the health of ecosystems. Recently, a middle school teacher was addressing this benchmark during a unit on endangered species. Much classroom discussion was devoted to salmon restoration. The goal of instruction was for students to identify human behaviors that affect salmon habitats. Equal amounts of time were spent on the salmon life cycle, the habitats in which salmon live at different phases of their life, and human behaviors that affect salmon habitats. The teacher wants to make up a test that will measure students' mastery of the benchmark and indicator. Here is one set of questions a teacher could ask:

1. Name three phases of the life cycle of the Chinook salmon.
2. Which of the following is not a habitat in which salmon live at some point in their life?
   (a) deep ocean
   (b) estuary
   (c) warm pond
   (d) cool stream
3. What is runoff?

Here is another item that would test the same content:

Imagine you are living in the year 2070. Your favorite thing to do is to go fishing, and your favorite fish to catch is Coho salmon, a species that

(Continued)

Box 4.1 (Continued)

is native to your area. Coho are abundant in the streams in your area, along with many other species of fish, such as Steelhead, Rainbow trout, and Chinook salmon. You know that back in the year 2000, salmon were on the endangered species list, but today they are thriving. Which of the following situations do you suppose most contributed to the health of native salmon in the year 2070?

(a) Many salmon hatcheries were developed and farm-raised salmon were released at sea.
(b) Strict limits were placed on agricultural, commercial, and industrial development along streams where salmon breed.
(c) Genetic engineering led to development of more disease-resistant salmon.

Write a short essay explaining your answer.

The first three items, which require reiteration or summarization, are indirect tasks because students are never asked to demonstrate an understanding of the effects of human behavior on salmon habitats, the stated goals of instruction. Students simply need to recall declarative information stored in long-term memory and produce it in the same format in which it was learned. The last item, which requires students to use information more actively, is a direct measure of students' thinking. To respond to this item, students need to use declarative information (life cycle of salmon, effects of human behavior) as well as conditional knowledge, (i.e., the principle "the more development that occurs along streams, the less healthy the salmon population becomes"). Any of the three choices could be correct, and each could be supported with information that was provided during instruction. However, students' presentation of a rationale for a particular choice would provide a more direct measure of their thinking and understanding.

In its purest form, performance assessment involves a judge observing and subjectively evaluating an individual who actually is carrying out an activity, such as solving a problem. Performance assessment has been used for years in athletic competitions such as gymnastics or figure skating, as well as in the performing arts. Anyone who has ever watched the Olympics is familiar with this assessment strategy. In classrooms, where learning and thinking are largely covert or "inside the head" activities, performance assessment often focuses on products rather than activities. For examples, students may build a model structure, such as a bridge or tower, and then write an explanation of the calculations and steps involved. Such products are intended to tap multiple skills across disciplines. It is assumed that the quality of the product is a reflection of the quality of the thinking that underlies it.

Performance assessments used for IEP development should provide information about how the student accomplishes a task. There is a wide range of behaviors that might be elicited through performance assessment, but for IEP planning, those that require an extended constructed response that results in a permanent product are likely to be the most useful because they can be a rich source of evidence about the student's functioning in the general curriculum. For example, if a student is asked to generate a written story, the performance measures should provide information about the entire writing process the student employs, from planning and prewriting to the final draft. Similarly, a math performance task should provide information about the problem-solving strategies the student uses in addition to the accuracy of her or his work, while a science task should provide information about a student's use of scientific inquiry. It is helpful for teachers to examine student work samples to gain an understanding of what constitutes a good performance on a task; this can help direct teachers to the skills that students may need to gain.

Previously, we discussed the various types of information that are contained in the general curriculum (facts, concepts, principles, procedures, strategies). We showed the distinctions among facts, concepts, principles, and procedures in Figure 2.2. The format of the information contained in the curriculum determines the kind of thinking required to use it. The more complex the information is, the more useful it is for complex thinking and problem solving. Simple information, such as facts and concrete concepts, can only be used in simple thinking processes (e.g., verbatim reiteration). The various cognitive operations that can be performed with facts, concepts, and principles are shown in Figure 4.1. The information in Figure 4.1 is based on a taxonomy developed by Williams and Haladyna (1982), as well as the classic work of Bloom and colleagues (1956).

Performance assessments used for IEP planning generally will have three necessary components: indicators, prompts, and performance criteria.

Indicators. The curriculum frameworks based on content standards usually are organized hierarchically, often in three levels. The top level usually specifies the standard, indicating a general, overarching class of knowledge and skills. At the next level, benchmarks indicate an intermediate level of specificity that further defines the standard. Three or more benchmarks typically are provided for each standard. At the lowest level are indicators or criteria. The indicators are the most specific and immediate components of the standard, and they define the various skills and knowledge subcomponents that a student is expected to master. Multiple indicators usually are provided for each benchmark, and separate benchmarks and indicators usually are developed for each grade level. Figure 4.2 shows examples of standards and benchmarks listed in the Essential Academic Learning Requirements (EALRs) for mathematics in Washington state.

The benchmark and indicators tell specifically what a student must do to demonstrate proficiency on a standard. Performance assessments that yield useful information for the IEP team generally will be constructed at the indicator

Figure 4.1 Cognitive Operations for Three Kinds of Information

	Cognitive Activities Required for Each Type of Information		
Cognitive Operation	***Facts***	***Concepts***	***Principles***
Reiterate	Verbatim reproduction of the information presented during instruction. *Example:* "Albany is the capital of New York."	Verbatim reproduction of the concept name and defining attributes. *Example:* "A triangle is a three-sided polygon."	Verbatim reproduction of the rule. *Example:* "If you heat a gas, it will expand."
Summarize	Reproduce the fact in a slightly different form. *Example:* "The capital of New York is Albany."	Reproduce the concept name and defining attributes in a different form. *Example:* "A shape that has only three sides is a triangle."	Reproduce the rule in a different form. *Example:* "Heating a gas will cause it to expand."
Illustrate	Can't be done.	Recognize or generate an example not previously encountered. *Example:* Student draws a triangle when asked to do so.	Provide or recognize an example that shows the relationship stated in the rule. *Example:* Student observes balloon burst when held over candle, then states the rule.
Predict	Can't be done.	Tell what will happen in another setting or at some point in the future. Can only be done with some concepts. *Example*: Teacher removes one side of a square made of sticks and asks the student to tell what will be created if the remaining sticks are joined. Student replies, "A triangle."	Tell what will happen, given the first part of the rule. *Example*: Teacher asks, "What do you think will happen if we hold this bottle over the burner?" Student replies, "The air inside will expand and make the cork fly off."

Figure 4.2 State of Washington Mathematics Essential Academic Learning Requirements and Benchmarks for Grade 7

Mathematics Content Standards	*Benchmarks for Grade 7*
Standard 1: The student understands and applies the concepts and procedures of mathematics.	
1.2 Understand and apply concepts and procedures from measurement: *attributes and dimensions*	• Understand the relationship among perimeter, area, and volume • Measure objects and events directly, or use indirect methods, such as finding the area of a rectangle given its length and width • Understand the concept of rate and how to calculate rates and determine units
Standard 4: The student communicates knowledge and understanding in both everyday and mathematical language	
4.1 *Gather information*	• Develop and follow a plan for collecting information • Use reading, listening, and observation to access and extract mathematical information from multiple sources, such as pictures, diagrams, physical models, oral narratives, and symbolic representations
4.3 *Represent and share information*	• Clearly and effectively express or present ideas and situations using both everyday and mathematical language, such as models, tables, charts, graphs, written reflection, or algebraic notation • Explain or represent mathematical ideas in ways appropriate for audience and purpose

Figure 4.3 Basketball Court Prompt

Today you are going to work on a problem about planning a basketball court. You will be evaluated on how well you understand measurement, how well you communicate your ideas and understanding, and the accuracy of your work. You may use a ruler and a calculator in your work. Read the problem in the box:

"The Basketball Court"

Hanna and Anthony are setting up a basketball court in a parking lot near their school. The school will set up the basketball hoops, but the students need to lay out the court. Here is what the rule book says about the dimensions and markings for the court:

> *The court should be 30 yards long and 16 yards wide. A midcourt line should be marked out across the center of the court. The center circle should be marked halfway along this line This circle should be 4 yards in diameter. The location for the poles that will hold the baskets should be centered at each end of the court.*

Hanna has a spool of string and a 50-foot measuring tape showing feet and inches.

1. Draw a diagram on the graph paper to show how Hanna and Anthony can use her 50-foot tape and the string to plan the basketball court. Label each part of your drawing and each of the steps Hanna and Anthony will follow.
2. On lined paper, write a description of the steps Hanna and Anthony might take to set up the basketball court.

level. For example, a performance assessment based on the first standard in Figure 4.2 might require students to calculate the area of a rectangular garden plot, given its perimeter.

Prompts. The prompt is the actual question or problem that is presented to the students, and it clearly identifies the expected outcomes for the assessment. The prompt should explicitly tell students what they are expected or encouraged to do to complete the task and what documentation or products are to be generated. The prompt also should communicate the relevance of the task by providing a context for the problem, as in a short scenario that "sets up" the task. The basketball court prompt in Figure 4.3 provides an example of a prompt that possesses all of these characteristics.

It is critical to verify that the desired content and skills are assessed by the prompt. The IEP team should develop a task description that delineates the following information:

1. The indicators that will be addressed by the performance measure
2. The specific content knowledge and skills to be assessed
3. A description of the student's activities and behaviors and the products that will be produced
4. The materials and resources the student will need to complete the task
5. A clear description of the correct solution or exemplars of acceptable products to be generated, which should be based on the performance of

a typical general education grade-level peer (The task should permit multiple correct responses that make visible the student's thinking and problem solving relative to the standard being assessed.)

6. An accurate estimate of the time a typical grade-level peer would require to complete the task (The IEP team should estimate the amount of time the target student would likely need to complete the task and whether the student will need more time than would be required by a typical student.)

7. A clear description of the level of support that will be provided by a teacher or other students for completion of the task (Ideally, the task should provide a picture of the student's unaided performance and not reflect the knowledge of other students or a teacher or paraprofessional who may be working with the student.)

Figure 4.4 shows an example of a task description for the performance task corresponding to the Basketball Court prompt, based on the state of Washington's EALRs.

Performance Criteria. Classroom-based performance assessments require a systematic process for determining which performances should be observed and for clearly articulating the criteria for judging the performance. Performance criteria often are formatted as scoring rubrics or rating scales that communicate the continuum of competence against which the student's performance will be judged. Look again at the example shown in Box 4.1. The first three items in the example would be scored as either "right" or "wrong," but the last item would be judged on a continuum, or scale of competence, based on the accuracy of the information as well as the strength of the argument used. Scaling implies that thinking and understanding can exist to varying degrees rather than in a "can or can't" dichotomy. It is assumed that all students would be able to engage in some level of complex thinking about salmon habitats, but some likely would have a more complete understanding and be able to use that knowledge more effectively.

A rubric is a set of scoring guidelines that describe a range of possible responses to a particular assessment item. Generally, a rubric contains a scale that indicates the points that will be assigned to a student's work and a set of descriptors for each point on that scale. Scales of 3, 4, or 5 points commonly are used in schools, with the highest value on the scale representing the most proficient performance.

When scoring rubrics are employed in accountability assessments, students often are judged as having "met" or "not met" a particular performance standard embedded in the rubrics. Often, a 3-point scale is used, with the midpoint indicating "at standard," the highest point indicating "above standard," and the lowest point "below standard." However, for IEP planning, rubrics should be framed to provide diagnostic information about the essential elements of the typical student's performance. Each of the anchor points on the scale should be

Figure 4.4 Task Description for the Basketball Court Problem

Indicators or Benchmarks assessed	**Math EALR 1.2 Grade 7 Benchmark**: Measure objects and events directly or use indirect methods such as finding the area of a rectangle given its length and width.
Content knowledge and skills to be assessed	• Interpret vocabulary (e.g., rectangle, circle, halfway, center). • Understand relationships among units and convert from one unit to another within the same system. • Select and apply techniques and tools to accurately find length and diameter.
Student activities and behaviors	Student will draw a diagram and describe a strategy for laying out a basketball court, given a description of the dimensions and markings for the court. Student will write an explanation of steps involved in the task and provide a rationale for decisions.
Products that will be produced	Graphic representation of solution Written explanation (2–3 paragraphs)
Materials and resources needed	Graph paper (5 squares/inch) Inch ruler Pencil Lined paper Calculator
Description of correct solutions	Correct responses will show an accurate representation of the basketball court, showing the midcourt line, center circle, and location for the baskets. Written explanation will illustrate accurate conversions between yards and feet and a cogent description of the steps necessary to complete the task. Rationale will be based on use of appropriate measurement and conversion strategies and use of procedures for computing perimeter and area.
Time a typical grade-level peer would require to complete the task	45 minutes for completion of all steps
Support that will be provided by a teacher or other students	Teacher will read directions.

NOTE: EALR = Essential Academic Learning Requirement

accompanied by an explicit description of what performance at that level of proficiency looks like, with the highest end of the scale representing the performance of a competent general education grade-level peer. There should be a direct relationship among descriptors at various points on the scale. Generally, a meaningful continuum can be communicated with a 4-point scale, depending on the complexity of the performance being evaluated.

There are two general categories of rubrics: holistic and analytic.

With holistic scoring, a quick overall impression of a student's work is formed and then compared with exemplars or "range finders" that represent various levels of competence. Some general procedures for creating holistic rubrics are shown in Box 4.2. Holistic rubrics can be developed quickly and provide information about the range of performance within a particular group of students; however, holistic rubrics do not necessarily provide information about student performance relative to specific curriculum outcomes. Work samples are rated only in comparison with all other samples in the group, so it is possible that even the best sample in the group may not be particularly good when compared with an external standard. This is why analytic rubrics are a more useful tool for making decisions about student performance relative to content and performance standards.

Analytic rubrics provide a set of predetermined statements that clearly describe performance corresponding to each point on the scale. These statements are established before student work is evaluated and are intended to describe clearly the continuum of competence along which a learner would move to become more proficient. Figures 4.5 and 4.6 show a set of rubrics for evaluating mathematics problem solving.

Box 4.2 Procedures for Creating Holistic Scoring Rubrics

Here are the general procedures that Tindal and Marston (1990) suggest for developing holistic scoring rubrics:

1. Quickly review all of the samples of work in the group and identify one or two range finders corresponding to each point on the scale you wish to develop. For example, if you want a 4-point scale, you might identify eight exemplars—two for each point on the scale.
2. Examine the range finders and decide which characteristics of the work make it an example of the scale value it is intended to represent. For example, if you are evaluating writing samples, decide which aspects characterize the "4" papers, what distinguishes the "3" papers from the "2" papers, and so on.
3. Develop a summary description of the attributes that distinguish each anchor point on the scale.
4. Examine the remainder of the work samples in the group and compare them with the range finders and the summary descriptions of each scale value. Assign each of the remaining work samples a score, based on the range finder it most closely resembles.

Figure 4.5 Scoring Rubric for Mathematics Problem Solving

Score	*Problem-Solving Interpretation*
3	The student has identified all critical dimensions of the problem. The problem has been accurately decomposed, and multiple solution strategies have been identified. All computations are accurate, and a cogent rationale or explanation is provided.
2	The student has identified most key dimensions of the problem. More than one solution may be suggested, but elaboration is incomplete or lacks cogency. The problem is generally decomposed effectively, although there may be some minor omissions or inaccurate assumptions represented. Computations are generally accurate. Rationale or explanations are generally, but not completely, accurate or logical.
1	The student has identified only the most superficial or obvious problem dimensions. Only one solution is presented. Problem decomposition is incomplete or based on misrules or false assumptions. The solution contains errors that directly affect outcomes and conclusions. Rationale or explanations are minimal or absent.

Figure 4.6 Example of Analytic Scoring Rubric for "Representing the Problem in a Diagram"

Score	*Representing the Problem in a Diagram Interpretation*
3	The student has accurately and effectively diagramed the problem. The diagram is drawn to appropriate scale, and all elements are accurately and appropriately placed within the diagram.
2	The diagram of the problem is generally effective. The scale or dimensions may be inaccurately drawn, or a few elements are missing or misplaced.
1	The diagram presents only an approximation of the problem. Scale or dimensions may be inaccurate or otherwise indicate that the student has not accurately interpreted the problem. Key elements or details are missing.

Well-designed analytic rubrics can provide clear criteria for evaluating student performance when they are tied directly to curriculum outcomes

Here are some general characteristics of well-designed scoring rubrics:

- Rubrics used to monitor progress in the general curriculum should be linked directly to clearly stated curriculum standards. Effective rubrics often include related benchmarks or indicators.
- Well-defined rubrics use descriptive language that focuses on the key feature of performance being considered. It should be readily apparent in the rubric which dimension of performance is being evaluated.
- Effective rubrics clearly indicate a continuum of proficiency, ranging from novice to expert. There should be a direct relationship among descriptors at various points on the scale.
- A single rubric should focus on only one dimension of performance. When more than one dimension is important, separate rubrics should be

used for each. For example, a separate rubric would be needed to scale "communicating about math problem solving" because communication skills are not addressed in the rubrics in Figure 4.5 and 4.6.

- Well-designed rubrics include enough scale points to allow meaningful discrimination among levels of proficiency but not so many as to make scoring unreliable. Generally, rubrics should contain no fewer than 3 points and no more than 7 points. A "zero" point should be included to differentiate no performance from very novice performance.
- Effective rubrics focus on the outcome of performance rather than the process a student uses. The emphasis should be on evidence of proficiency rather than effort expended. For example, it usually is not very useful to design rubrics to scale student effort or the extent to which a student enjoys or appreciates an activity. Although these may be instructionally relevant variables, they may not be valid indicators of performance.
- Rubrics should be shared with students while they are in the process of learning the skills or knowledge that will later be evaluated with the rubric. This strategy clearly communicates what the student will be expected to do to demonstrate proficiency and what dimensions of performance the teacher values. Rubric descriptors should be easily interpreted and meaningful to the student.

Performance criteria (i.e., a scoring rubric) should be developed for each of the indicators the performance assessment is intended to address. Also, separate rubrics may be needed for various metacognitive or problem-solving processes that may be of interest, such as "use of scientific inquiry," "planning to write," or "decomposing word problems." Well-designed scoring rubrics will provide the first level of diagnostic information about the student's performance on the standard. When a student performs below standard, the team typically will need to collect additional information about various aspects of performance that might be addressed through accommodations or modifications.

It may be useful to develop brief probes to collect information about specific behaviors or areas of knowledge. These are mini-performance assessments that may take from 5 to 20 minutes for the student to complete; these assessments tap a critical aspect of performance that may be a candidate for an accommodation or modification. Figure 4.7 shows some examples of performance dimensions, probe procedures, and possible accommodations that might be indicated based on the results of the probes.

IN WHAT WAYS IS THE STUDENT'S DISABILITY IMPACTING ACADEMIC ACHIEVEMENT AND FUNCTIONAL PERFORMANCE IN THE GENERAL EDUCATION CURRICULUM?

At times, the impact of a student's disability on academic achievement is quite obvious. Clearly, a student who has sensory or mobility deficits will require supports aimed at compensating for those deficits. However, one of the most persistent problems that IEP teams face is that often it is very difficult to separate the

Figure 4.7 Performance Dimensions, Probes, and Accommodations

Dimension	***Assessment***	***Probe***	***Accommodation***
Fluency	Is the student able to perform quickly and accurately?	• Parallel forms of performance tasks, timed and untimed. • Compare accuracy.	• Allow more time when accuracy counts.
Prior Knowledge	Does the student lack prior knowledge necessary to complete a performance task? Is the student activating prior knowledge?	• Teach necessary prior knowledge for the task, and then administer the task.	• Provide prior knowledge "crib sheets."
Self-Regulation and Strategic Knowledge	Does the student have or use effective self-regulation and problem-solving strategies?	• Provide incentives for error checking. • Administer "think aloud" performance tasks. • Provide explicit directions to employ strategies, and then score accuracy.	• Provide metacognitive supports within the context of class work, such as mnemonic prompts, problem-solving flow charts, or assignments formatted to prompt self-regulation.
Perseverance	Does the student stay with tasks to completion?	• Break tasks into small steps and observe overall outcomes. • Present a series of tasks of increasing length and complexity and record "break point."	• Break tasks into small chunks. • Provide incentives for completion of subcomponents.
Presentation Modes	Does the student acquire information differently in different modes?	• Present parallel tasks in different modes (e.g., oral and written instructions) and observe outcomes.	• Use universal design principles in creating materials.
Response Modes	Does the student perform differently with different response modes?	• Elicit parallel responses in different modes and observe outcomes.	• Use universal design principles in creating materials.

direct impact of disability from other factors that impact school performance, such as language, class, previous educational opportunity, culture, or various family factors. This dilemma is particularly problematic for teams attempting to sort out the needs of students labeled as "learning disabled" because often the primary criteria for serving students in special education under this category is the existence of an IQ-achievement discrepancy. The mere presence of a gap between a student's score on an IQ test and her or his score on an achievement test provides no instructionally relevant information on which to build an educational program. For example, research during the last decade has shown that often, young, poor readers who have an IQ-achievement discrepancy perform no differently than young poor readers who do not demonstrate such a discrepancy (Fuchs, Mock, Morgan, & Young, 2003).

Recently, a number of professional organizations, including the Council for Exceptional Children, the National Association of School Psychologists, and the National Association of State Directors of Special Education, have advocated for an approach in which IEP teams focus on a student's *responsiveness to intervention* (RTI) in the general education curriculum when determining whether a student needs special education and when designing individualized educational programs. Additionally, the 2004 IDEA includes specific wording requiring the provision of "appropriate instruction" in reading as defined by NCLB. Generally, an RTI approach involves the following elements:

1. Students receive a high quality educational program in their general education classroom. High quality programs usually are research validated and generally effective with most students.
2. Student progress is monitored continuously. Curriculum-based measures often are used for this purpose. We will discuss curriculum-based assessment in the next section.
3. Those students who fail to make progress, as evidenced during routine monitoring, are provided with additional instructional support, which is often described as differing in intensity from the instruction that most students receive (Barnett, Daly, Jones, & Lenz, 2004). This additional support might take the form of additional instructional time or involvement of professionals other than the classroom teacher.
4. Students who still do not make progress might be found eligible for special education or for special education evaluation.

There are two broad approaches to implementing RTI. One approach assumes that the general education teachers and administrators are engaged in some form of problem-solving process that seeks to identify instructional and student variables that could explain poor performance and then develop appropriate plans to remediate those problems. Often problem solving is associated with pre-referral intervention and consulting models of special education delivery.

The second broad approach to RTI assumes the instruction being provided in the general education classroom is effective and implemented with fidelity. In fact, IDEA (PL 108–446) requires that the interventions used with students with disabilities be based on *peer-reviewed research* to the extent practicable. The implication is that it would be inappropriate to categorize students as having a disability if they have not had sufficient opportunity or exposure to instruction with proven effectiveness. Some programs that have implemented RTI have employed standard protocols in which all students in a particular setting receive the same empirically validated intervention. For example, students who fail to make progress in reading in first grade might receive an intensive program of direct, explicit phonics-based reading instruction. Advocates of a standard protocol approach argue that if the intervention has been rigorously validated by research, large numbers of students would participate in an effective instructional program, and thus fewer would be erroneously referred to special education.

Common to the various models of RTI are attributes that can be adopted by an IEP team attempting to both determine the impact of a student's disability and identify accommodations and modifications that will help the student make progress in the general curriculum. We'll discuss them briefly here.

1. **Multiple levels of student-focused interventions that vary in intensity.** The basic requirements of this strategy include task analysis of the academic performances in which the student is failing to make progress and systematic intervention focused on that task analysis. Continuous progress monitoring is used to evaluate the direct effects of intervention changes.

2. **Interventions that are varied systematically on the dimensions of instructional intensity: duration, frequency, and time.** The assumption is that the instructional program being implemented in the general education classroom is of high quality and generally effective for most students. Therefore, when a particular student fails to make progress, the first level of inquiry focuses on the intensity of the intervention rather than core characteristics of the instructional program. For example, if the general education mathematics program includes some instruction on basic operations, the IEP team might increase the amount of time each day or number of times each week that the student receives instruction on basic mathematics operations. Then, if the student begins to show growth on progress monitoring measures, (e.g., math facts probes), it could be inferred that the more intensive instructional program was effective.

3. **Implementation of a differentiated curriculum.** It is assumed that something different is going to be done for students who fail to make progress. If a "one size fits all" curriculum is expected to fit all students, it is going to be very difficult to determine whether a student's lack of progress is the result of the disability or the curriculum.

4. **Instructional supports that are provided by staff other than, or in addition to, the classroom teacher.** The time and resources required to find out how well a student is responding to a particular intervention generally are greater than a classroom teacher has available.

It must be noted that RTI is not without controversy. Concerns have been raised about the wide scale implementation of RTI as a strategy for making eligibility decisions or in settings where fidelity of implementation of instructional programs cannot be tightly controlled (Gerber, 2003). However, to the extent that RTI focuses on both interventions that can be implemented in general education classrooms and academic achievement of all students in the general education curriculum, we believe it is an approach that could provide valuable information for IEP planning teams. Moreover, this approach is supported by language in the 2004 IDEA.

IS THE STUDENT MAKING PROGRESS IN THE GENERAL EDUCATION CURRICULUM?

Evaluating student progress in the general curriculum involves use of multiple assessment strategies. No single measure will provide enough information. Therefore, it is important for teachers to see how various assessment procedures fit together.

The first step in determining whether a student is making progress is to identify the reference standard against which progress will be measured. A reference standard is simply a known unit to which the thing being measured can be compared or "referenced." A tape measure used to measure a piece of lumber is a standard, as is a measuring cup used to measure ingredients in a recipe. In education, three types of standards commonly are used: **norm**, **criterion**, and **individual**. Norm referencing involves comparison of the performance of an individual with that of a particular group. Criterion referencing entails comparison of the performance of an individual with an objective or with a performance standard such as a scoring rubric or rating scale. Individual referencing involves comparison of a student's performance on a task at one point in time with their previous performance on the same task. These three reference standards are discussed in the sections that follow.

Norm-Referenced Decisions

Norm-referenced assessment tools are useful whenever it is important to know how a particular student or group of students compares with a reference or norm group. Norm referencing allows an evaluator to make a judgment about whether a particular student is "different." The further an individual's scores fall from average, usually, the mean of the norm group, the more different the individual is considered to be. For example, if an IEP team is interested in knowing whether a particular student is catching up to her or his peers, norm-referenced measures would provide information about the gap between that student's performance and that of the norm group.

Most published norm-referenced tests such as the Iowa Test of Basic Skills (Hoover, Hieronymus, Frisbie, & Dunbar, 1993), or the Terra Nova CAT/6 (CTB McGraw-Hill, 2000) are normed on a large sample of subjects who take various versions of the test while it is being developed. Test items are modified, added, and deleted during this development process until the distribution of scores obtained by the norm group takes the form of a normal distribution. This is the familiar shape commonly referred to as a "bell curve." Because norm referencing requires use of standardized administration and scoring procedures to ensure that everyone who takes the test does so under the same conditions, these tests commonly are referred to as "standardized tests."

The statistical properties of normal distributions are what make possible the kind of norm-referenced decision making with which most educators are familiar. All normal distributions are symmetrical, with approximately 68% of the cases falling within plus or minus one standard deviation of the mean and approximately 96% of the cases falling within plus or minus two standard deviations of the mean. A score that is one standard deviation below the mean is lower than about 84% of the people in the norm group who took the test. For example, if a person obtains a score of 70 on a norm-referenced intelligence test that has a mean of 100 and a standard deviation of 15, only about 16% of the people who take the test are likely to get a lower score. Many educators would consider this performance "different enough" to make the individual eligible for special education.

Standardized tests frequently are used to evaluate school performance. This is accomplished by comparing scores of the students in a school with those of the national norm group. However, these tests are not linked to a particular set of outcomes or standards, nor are they based on any particular curriculum materials. Therefore, it is possible for all of the students in a school to score above the mean of their respective norm groups but still not make progress toward local curriculum goals.

While decisions about eligibility for special education tend to rely on norm-referenced measures, norm referencing is of limited utility for making judgments about a student's progress in the general curriculum. Norm referencing cannot provide useful information about a student's present level of academic achievement or functional performance in a particular skill or content area, nor can norm-referenced assessment help a teacher decide what a student needs to learn next. Questions of this type can only be answered through use of criterion-referenced measures.

Criterion-Referenced Decisions

Criterion-referenced evaluation involves comparison of the performance of an individual with the characteristics of a particular domain. Early use of criterion-referenced testing often involved lists of objectives thought to represent competent performance in a particular skill or content area. A set of test items was developed to test each objective, and the more items a student passed, the more of the domain they were thought to have mastered. Pass/no pass criteria usually were established on the basis of the expert judgment of the test developer or through some normative process.

The school accountability measures in wide use today are a variation on the theme of criterion-referenced testing. Today, however, domains such as reading, writing, and math are represented by curriculum standards, benchmarks, and indicators rather than discrete instructional objectives. Schools often are evaluated on the basis of the number of students who successfully master or reach a set level of proficiency on the various curriculum standards as measured by state assessments.

Standards-referenced assessments are designed to determine whether a student is making progress in the general curriculum. Over time, students whose educational programs are effective would be expected to demonstrate proficiency on a greater proportion of the curriculum content standards. Students who fail to demonstrate such growth over time would not be viewed as making progress in the general curriculum.

A word of caution is in order when interpreting standards-based performance measures. The points on a rubric only represent mileposts along a continuum of competence; rubrics are not equal interval scales. The difference between performance that is scored "1" and performance that is scored "2" may be much greater than the difference between "4" and "5" performance. Also, rubrics may not be very sensitive to growth that occurs in less than 4 to 6 months if they are intended to reference larger curriculum outcomes rather than short-term instruction. Even under optimal instructional conditions, it may take a student months to move up a single point on a rubric scale. Of course, if the instruction is not effective, it will take even longer. In any case, if a teacher uses only rubrics to measure growth, an unacceptable amount of time will pass before the teacher discovers that a particular student is not progressing in the general curriculum. This is the main reason we suggest that IEP teams use criterion-referenced performance assessment in conjunction with individual-referenced evaluation.

Individual-Referenced Decision Making

Individual-referenced decision making involves systematic comparisons of students' current work with their previous performance. Individual-referenced evaluation often is referred to as "formative evaluation" because the effects of instruction are evaluated on an ongoing basis rather than after all instruction has been delivered. Instruction is modified whenever the evaluation indicates that students are not learning. Individual-referenced evaluation tools tell whether a student is making progress toward specific outcomes that are subcomponents of larger curriculum outcomes.

Individual-referenced evaluation often has been used to monitor progress toward special education IEP goals, using procedures associated with curriculum-based measurement (CBM). CBM is a well-researched strategy for collecting individual-referenced data and is an integral part of RTI approaches. Originally developed by Stanley Deno and associates at the University of Minnesota Institute for Research on Learning Disabilities, CBM has been found to be a technically adequate means for making data-based decisions about student learning, primarily in the basic skills of reading, written expression, math computation, and spelling. With CBM, students respond directly to brief probes that are sampled from the curriculum materials in use in their local classroom or school. Administration and scoring of CBM probes is standardized, and the criterion used to evaluate student performance is fluency rather than just accuracy.

Deno's (1985) original idea in developing CBM was for teachers to have a quick measure of students' academic vital signs, analogous to the measures of pulse, temperature, and blood pressure that medical practitioners use to monitor physical health. In reading, students read orally for 1 minute. In written expression, students write narrative essays for 3 to 5 minutes in response to story starters. In spelling, students write 10 to 15 words presented in rolling dictation. In math computation, students complete basic skills probes (addition, subtraction, multiplication, and division) for 3 to 5 minutes. At the secondary level, CBM has involved maze and vocabulary matching tasks sampled from content curriculum materials (Espin, Scierka, Skare, & Halverson, 1999). These measures use objective scoring procedures rather than the subjective rating scales we discussed in the last section. For example, reading might be scored as the total number of words read correctly in 1 minute, math as the total number of correct digits supplied, and written expression as the percentage of correctly spelled words or correct word sequences.

These measures are intended to provide a "quick and dirty" look at a student's educational performance rather than the more extensive evaluation of thinking and learning processes that comes with performance assessment. If a student's vital signs are acceptable, no further assessment is merited. However, if these quick checks indicate a student is having difficulty, a more extensive evaluation will be undertaken.

Teachers usually make this quick assessment through visual analysis of data or with the help of a computer program (Fuchs, 1998). A probe is administered each week, and the score is plotted on a graph such as the one shown in Figure 4.8.

This graph shows the percentage of words spelled correctly on a 5-minute writing probe administered once each week. In Week 1, the student spelled about 20% of the words in the essay correctly. By Week 9, the student spelled about 35% of the words on the probe correctly. The dashed line is an aimline representing the long-term goal for the student. If this graph were drawn to show the entire school year, the aimline would show the slope of progress necessary to move from the student's level of performance at the beginning of the year to the level of performance indicated in the student's annual goal. In this case, the long-term goal is for the student to spell 100% of the words on the writing probe correctly.

Aimlines assist in development of decision rules to evaluate the effectiveness of instruction. Here is a typical decision rule: "Whenever progress is below the aimline for three consecutive data points, a change of instruction is indicated; whenever the student's progress is above the aimline for three consecutive data points, a more ambitious goal is developed." According to this decision rule, the data illustrated in the graph in Figure 4.8 indicate that change in instruction is needed. Even though the student has made steady progress, performance has been below the aimline for 4 consecutive weeks. If this rate of growth is projected out for the entire school year, the student will not achieve the annual goal of spelling 100% of the words correctly on the 5-minute writing probe. If the student's performance had been above the aimline for the last 3 or 4 weeks, the teacher would have written a new goal (e.g., "All words spelled

Figure 4.8 Individual-Referenced Data

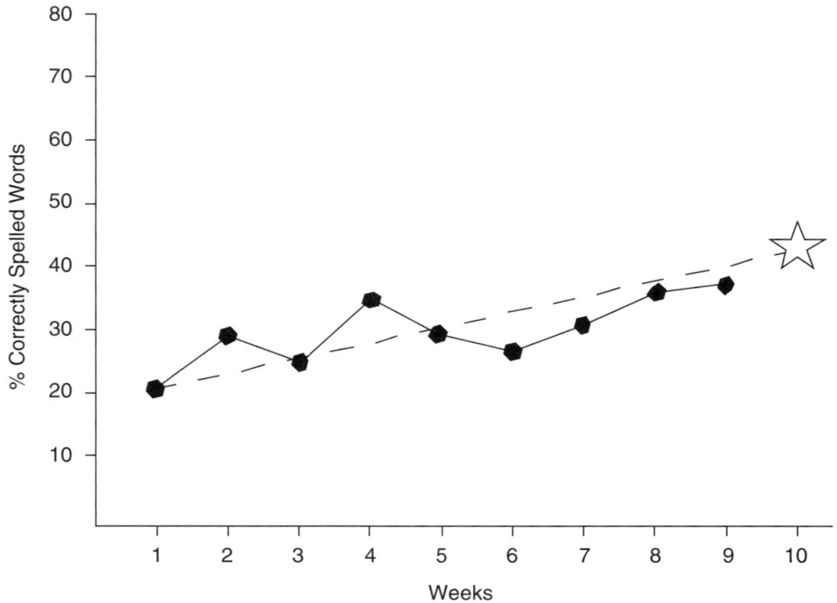

This graph shows progress in reading for one student over a 10-week period. Each data point corresponds to the percentage of words spelled correctly on weekly spelling tests. During Week 1, the student spelled 20% of the words correctly. By Week 9, the student spelled 29% of the words correctly. The dashed line with the star at the end shows the rate of progress represented in a 10-week objective. Only two of the weekly data points are above this "aimline," and all the rest are below. This indicates that the student did not accomplish the 10-week spelling objective.

correctly and no more than three errors of punctuation or capitalization on the 5-minute writing task").

Individual-referenced evaluation generally focuses on subcomponents or prerequisite skills of larger curriculum goals and benchmarks. For example, math problem solving requires accurate computation. If computation errors consistently contribute to a student's poor performance on math problem solving, a teacher may choose to monitor this single dimension of a student's performance with weekly math computation probes. Similarly, a teacher may choose to monitor a student's reading proficiency (clearly a preskill needed for most complex performance tasks), using weekly oral reading fluency probes. If it is clear from individual-referenced evaluation that a student is not making sufficient growth in computation or reading fluency, a teacher will make an instructional change.

Here are the general procedures for using individual-referenced evaluation:

1. Identify the general outcome you wish to measure. These are subcomponents of larger curriculum goals. Examples include written expression, math problem solving, reading decoding or fluency for beginning readers, and reading comprehension for older readers. Often, the scope and sequence of curriculum materials can help guide this process.

2. Identify tasks that are key indicators of the general outcome. An indicator is not the general outcome expected; it is just a correlate. For example, oral reading fluency is correlated with other measures of reading (e.g., comprehension) and with teacher ratings. Similarly, computation might be an indicator of math problem solving. Short narrative essays might be an indicator of more general writing proficiency.

3. Find out the student's present level of academic achievement on the task you have chosen as an indicator of the general outcome. This step usually involves administration of one or more direct measures of the task. For example, you might determine a student's present level of academic achievement in math computation by administering a series of 2-minute addition, subtraction, multiplication, or division probes.

4. Identify a long-term goal for the outcome you wish to measure. Goals can be established normatively or through expert judgment. Local norms can be established with a small group of typical students at a particular grade level. For example, to find out what constitutes typical fourth-grade reading, you could ask the students in the middle reading group to read aloud for 1 minute from a passage they should read fluently by late January (or roughly the middle of the school year). It is possible to develop more precise and elaborate school or district norms using CBM, but the investment of resources necessary for this effort probably is not merited by the increase in precision that would be gained. When a student is performing below the grade level of the student's same-age peers, develop local norms across grade levels to establish useful goals.

5. Develop alternate forms of probes for the task to be measured. These probes must sample the goal material. For example, if the long-term goal for a student who currently is only 20% accurate in solving two- and three-digit subtraction problems is to solve them with 100% accuracy, the alternate forms of the probe would consist of two- and three-digit subtraction problems, regardless of the student's present instructional level. The idea is that over time, if instruction is effective, the student will make steady progress toward the goal. If measurement were conducted using only single-digit subtraction facts, the student would soon outgrow the measurement tool. The analogy here is the measuring tape attached to the wall of a child's bedroom. If the tape is only 3 feet long, the child will eventually outgrow it, and a new tape will be needed. The idea in developing probes for individual-referenced evaluation is to select a long enough tape right from the start.

6. Administer the probes on a weekly basis, under standardized conditions. Be sure to use a different probe each week to avoid the effects of practice or memory. It is usually acceptable to use a probe again after about 2 months. Therefore, 12 to 15 versions usually would be needed for an entire school year. It is critical that each administration of the probe be the same, so that meaningful interpretations can be made. Obviously, if a student has 3 minutes to write one week and 10 minutes the next, it would be difficult to evaluate the meaning of differences in the two writing samples.

7. Plot weekly data on a graph that also includes an aimline. Visual analysis of data typically involves estimating the slope or trend of the line of best fit. This is a simple procedure that has been described frequently. For more information about this process, the reader should consult Tindal and Marston (1990) or Howell and Nolet (2000).

8. Evaluate after every 5 or 6 data points and apply decision rules. Usually, an instructional change is warranted whenever students are not making sufficient progress, and a more ambitious goal is developed whenever students exceed their aimlines.

Evaluating progress in the general curriculum requires an integrated evaluation program that combines all of these tools, but they don't all need to be used every day. Remember, never let teaching take a back seat to testing. ***When in doubt, teach.*** Testing is just a way to see if your teaching has been effective. Figure 4.9 shows a suggested schedule for using the tools we have been discussing to monitor the success of your students in the general education curriculum.

Figure 4.9 Suggested Schedule for Using Progress Monitoring Tools

Frequency	*Procedure*	*Purpose*
Every two or three years	State-mandated school accountability measures employing performance assessment and scoring rubrics.	Evaluate school effectiveness at teaching curriculum standards and benchmarks.
Once a year	Published, norm-referenced achievement tests.	Compare students in a particular school or classroom with a national norm sample.
Three to four times a year	Locally developed (district, school, or teacher) performance assessments linked to curriculum standards and benchmarks. Use scoring rubrics and monitor individual student progress.	Evaluate student use of complex thinking and problem solving contained in curriculum frameworks.
Once a month	Curriculum-based measures of larger subcomponent skills, such as written expression and math problem solving. Use objective scoring procedures and decision rules.	Monitor progress in skills that are subcomponents of larger curriculum outcomes.
Once a week	Curriculum-based measures of basic skills, such as oral reading fluency, math computation, or vocabulary. Use objective scoring procedures and decision rules.	Monitor progress in acquisition of basic skills associated with performance in larger domains.

5 Curriculum Access and the Individualized Education Program

The Individualized Education Program (IEP) is a written statement of an individually tailored education program that represents a child's entitlement to a "free and appropriate education." The IEP is the foundation of special education law and practice. The IEP is the tool for designing access to the general education curriculum for each student with a disability. An IEP must be developed annually for every student with a disability who receives special education and related services under the Individuals with Disabilities Education Act (IDEA). It must contain the measurable academic and functional goals to be achieved, as well as the specialized interventions that are to be provided. The IEP is to be based on a careful assessment of the individual student and should be the culmination of a planning process that is both multidisciplinary and family inclusive.

The IEP is intended to be used as an instructional planning tool and is focused on students' participation and progress in the general education standards and curriculum. These components include:

- A statement of the child's present levels of academic achievement and functional performance, specifying how the child's disability affects involvement and progress in the general education curriculum
- Measurable annual goals, and for a small group of students who may participate in alternate assessments and be held to alternate achievement standards, a description of short-term objectives or benchmarks that are designed to enable the child to be involved and make progress in the general education curriculum as well as other educational needs arising from the child's disability
- A statement of the special education and related services and supplementary aids and services (based on peer-reviewed research to the extent practical) that will be provided to the child

- Any program modifications or supports for school personnel necessary for the child to advance appropriately toward the annual goals, be involved and make progress in the general education curriculum, participate in extracurricular and other nonacademic activities, and be educated and participate with other children with or without disabilities
- An explanation of the extent, if any, to which the child will **not** participate with nondisabled children in regular class activities

The IEP must also include whatever accommodations a child will receive on the state (or district) assessments. If the IEP team determines that a child will take an alternate assessment on a particular state or district assessment, the team must document why the child cannot participate in the regular assessment and why the selected alternate assessment is appropriate for the child.

While the IEP focuses on how a student will access the general education curriculum, it does not denote the importance of making individual decisions about students and their instructional needs. The challenge for special educators is how to make those individualized decisions within the context of a common set of content and achievement standards that determine the general education curriculum. In this chapter and in Chapter 6, we will present a process for thinking about and deciding how a student will access the general education curriculum, and we will address each of the key IEP components.

A CONTINUUM OF CURRICULUM ACCESS

Access to the general education curriculum needs to be considered along the continuum we presented in Figure 1.1. We now explore that continuum a little further. The underlying premise of IDEA is that IEP planning for each child begins with the assumption that the student will be taught the subject matter as defined by the general education curriculum in the regular classroom. Decisions to make accommodations or modifications to the age-appropriate general education curriculum are made on the basis of evidence of a child's present level of performance and consideration of all supports and services. Two terms that are widely used in the development of IEPs are *accommodations* and *modifications* (sometimes also referred to as *adaptations*). It is important that teachers understand the differences between these two terms and how they apply to IEP decision making.

Some students who receive special education and related services may require no accommodations or modifications in a particular academic content area. They may be able to access the required general education curriculum content through the instruction that is provided within the general education classroom. This is the first level of the curriculum continuum. The next level of access on the continuum assumes that instructional accommodations will be made, but the student will be expected to learn the same amount of curriculum content at the same achievement level as the other students in the classroom. Curricular modifications begin to change one or more of the expectations regarding the specific content that is taught and the level of achievement that is expected. Finally, it is feasible that individualized goals referenced to the general education content standards—but to alternate achievement standards—may be defined for a very few students.

To understand the continuum, teachers must clearly understand the nature of the curriculum, as we discussed in Chapter 2, and be clear about the larger learning requirements associated with a subject matter content domain, as discussed in Chapter 3. Teachers must be able to differentiate curriculum *content* from *instruction*, have a firm understanding of a student's current level of performance, and know the difference between accommodations and modifications. Let's take a closer look at the continuum of curriculum access.

UNIVERSAL DESIGN FOR LEARNING AND ACCESS TO THE GENERAL EDUCATION CURRICULUM

The process of developing IEPs for students who have disabilities begins in the general education classroom. As we previously noted, the assumption underlying IDEA is that most if not all of the time, the accommodations, supports, and services required for a child with a disability to succeed can be provided through the general education curriculum within the general education classroom. For the majority of students served in special education, this assumption is correct. The gray band in Figure 5.1 shows where, on the continuum of supports, the program developed for those students would be located.

Notice that at this end of the continuum of supports, the student's instruction is almost entirely in the General Education Curriculum. Only a very small proportion of the student's program takes the form of Special Education and Related Services; perhaps the students receive only speech and language services, or perhaps the students receive instructional accommodations that are built into the curriculum. Educational programs located at this end of the curriculum support continuums that utilize a Universal Design for Learning (UDL). UDL can prevent the need for many specialized adaptations, and it should be the first response chosen by all teachers.

Figure 5.1 Curriculum Access Continuum

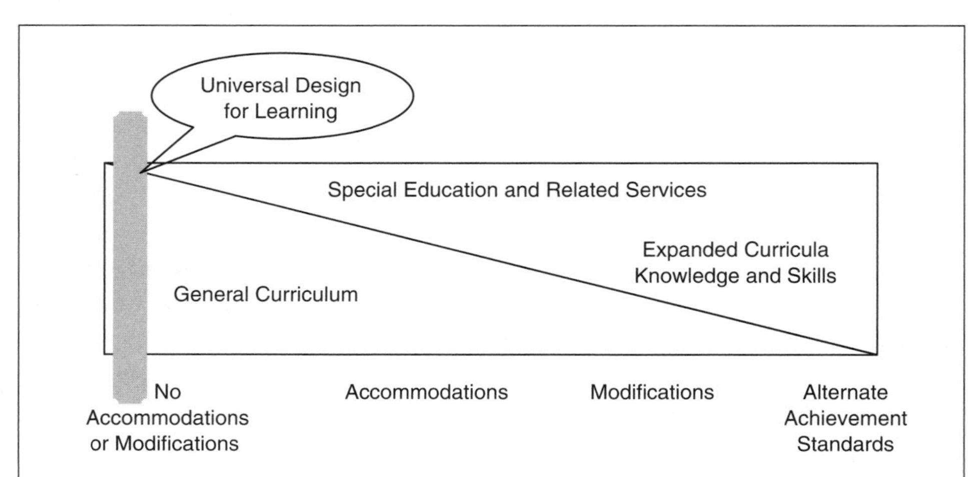

UDL refers to "designed-in" flexibility to accommodate the instructional needs of many diverse learners in a single classroom (Rose & Meyer, 2002). The underlying premise of UDL is that products and environments should be usable by the largest number of people possible without the need for additional modifications beyond those incorporated into the original design. When additional adaptations are needed, they should be easily and unobtrusively accommodated by the original design. Universal design implies that assistive supports are built in rather than added on as an afterthought.

Architectural applications of universal design such as curb cuts, automatic doors, and integrated ramps have become common in new construction in both public and private sectors. These features are now routinely included as integral elements during the design and blueprint phase of construction. Some nonexamples of universal design in architecture include features such as separate, disabled entrances or separate, handicapped accessible restrooms. Such add-on or separate features are required when designers fail to consider the likelihood that someone with limited mobility might wish to use the building. A much better alternative would be for the original design to include entrances that can be used by people who vary widely in terms of mobility and strength or restrooms with fixtures and clearances that do not preclude use by anyone.

UDL requires teachers to consider the critical effects of their instructional decisions on every student in the classroom, not just the mythical middle or "average" group. As the principles of universal design become integral to the overall design process, decisions that effectively limit access to, or use by, some individuals are replaced by designs that increase flexibility and accessibility for every student. For example, as more architects embrace the principles of universal design, graceful, well-integrated ramps have become commonplace in new construction, while door handles and other physical features in buildings are fully accessible and not some cobbled-together appendage.

One of the key benefits of universal design is that the built-in features that accommodate individuals with disabilities make it easier for everyone else to use the product or environment. For example, many household utensils and tools that are widely available in grocery and department stores have ergonomically designed handles. These tools are engineered to be used easily by individuals who have limited mobility or strength in their hands; however, they are popular because most people find them more comfortable than those with conventional handles. Indeed, most people who buy these products probably don't think of these utensils as "accessible."

Applications of the principles of universal design in educational contexts generally have focused on incorporating physical and sensory means of access, primarily in electronic media and in computer hardware and software. Most personal computers routinely include controls that allow the user to customize the speed of mouse and key commands, use alternative input keys, or turn auditory signals on and off. These capabilities are built into the operating system, not added on later as an adaptation, and they are readily available for anyone who may wish to use these features. Similarly, closed captioning decoders now are standard on most television sets, and this feature is used by many people other than those who are hard of hearing or deaf. It has become common to find televisions in noisy public areas such as restaurants and airport gates with closed captioning switched on.

One of the ways universal design accomplishes flexibility is through redundancy, that is, parallel systems that serve the same purpose. Access is increased when users can choose from among a range of options, those that best meet their needs or preferences. Stairs and ramps both serve the same purpose. Closed captioning accomplishes the same purpose as the audio track on a television program. The choice offered by these redundant or parallel systems creates accessibility.

The principles of universal design can readily be applied to the design of instruction that accommodates individuals with learning and cognitive disabilities. This type of UDL employs flexible curricular materials, such as digitalized textbooks, and activities that permit a wide range of learners to accomplish challenging learning outcomes. The Center for Applied Special Technology (Rose & Meyer, 2002) has summarized three essential principles of universal design for learning. Notice how the idea of flexibility through redundancy is central to these principles:

1. **Multiple means of representation.** This means that information should be available in more than one format. For example, captions should be provided for audio material, and relevant descriptors should be provided for graphics and video. Whenever possible, text should be provided in digital format, along with the printed version, to permit transformations of variables, such as size, color, shape, and spacing.

2. **Multiple means of expression.** This means that students should have comparable alternatives for communicating and demonstrating what they have learned and for interacting with the instructional system. For example, instead of writing a response with pencil and paper, a student could perform the same activity digitally, on a computer, orally, through speaking, or graphically through use of drawings, illustrations, or photography.

3. **Multiple means of engagement.** This means that all students are appropriately challenged by the content and format of the curriculum. For example, scaffolding is provided for those students who need it, and the amount of repetition built into instruction is matched to each student's rate of learning. At the same time, the instruction includes opportunities for all students to be challenged sufficiently for learning to occur.

UDL implies use of multiple ways for information to be represented, multiple ways for students to express themselves, and multiple pathways for students to be engaged in the curriculum. The purpose of building in this flexibility is to eliminate the effects of barriers to learning that are created when students have sensory, motor, cognitive, or language differences. The sections that follow provide specific strategies for incorporating the principles of universal design into day-to-day planning and teaching.

MULTIPLE MEANS OF REPRESENTATION

There is no single best way to present information to provide equal access for all learners. Indeed, a method that facilitates access for one individual may actually limit access for another. For example, a math lesson taught in Spanish would improve access for those students who speak Spanish as their first language but limit access for non-Spanish speakers. However, designs that build in flexibility through use of redundant or parallel systems will be less likely to present barriers than those designs that rely on a single representation strategy.

Teaching Presentations

Redundancy in teaching presentations means mentioning the same information more than once, in different ways. The grid in Figure 5.2 illustrates various ways teachers can employ more than one format for presenting information. Of course, it won't always be possible to present all information in redundant formats, but the more cells on the grid you can employ simultaneously, the more access will be built into your presentation. For example, if your primary mode for presenting new information is through lecture and discussion, then you could employ a video with captioning that presents the same information or construct a model to show key relationships.

Instructional Materials

As a general principle, designs that employ digital text are more desirable than those that rely only on printed text (Orkwis & McLane, 1998). Digital text is highly flexible because its shape, size, color, and contrast can be transformed easily to accommodate students whose perceptual or cognitive deficits interfere with their ability to obtain information from printed materials. While relatively few of the materials routinely used in classrooms are yet available in digital form, publishers and materials developers have recognized that there is a huge demand for instructional material in digital format. More instructional materials will soon be available in electronic form, either as stand-alone products or in networked environments.

Figure 5.2 Redundancy in Teaching Presentations

Redundant Representation Formats			
Say It	***Show It***	***Model It***	***Different Media***
lecture	pictures/graphics	demonstrate	videotape/-disc
discussion	transparency	think aloud	audiotape/-disc
questioning	white board	act out	computer
read aloud	video	build/construct	television
verbal descriptions	captions	manipulatives	manipulatives

In the meantime, there are some options available, albeit of the "plywood appendage" variety. Some instructional material can be scanned electronically and then presented to students in digital format, although this may not be an acceptable solution when the materials contain many graphics or unusual characters that cannot be interpreted by optical character recognition software.

When instructional materials include information presented in audio format (e.g., a videotape), redundancy should be built in through use of captioning or transcripts to enable students who have hearing impairments to gain access to the information. Similarly, when information is presented graphically or pictorially, verbal descriptions should be provided for those students who are blind or have low vision or who would benefit from more explicit presentations of material. The number and variety of video materials available with descriptive video is increasing rapidly and should be selected whenever possible.

MULTIPLE MEANS OF EXPRESSION

The principles of universal design imply that teachers should allow students to select, from a menu of options, the form of expression that best meets their needs. Here are some examples of alternative modes of expression students could use to express themselves throughout the learning process.

Presentation and Graphics Software

A number of computer software applications allow users to organize information into slides that can later be presented electronically, printed, or transformed into overhead transparencies. Using this software, learners who have difficulty either writing or speaking can express quite complex ideas and relationships with relatively little writing and no speaking. Using the clip-art, graphics, and formatting tools, users can even create polished products that contain no writing but readily express ideas and demonstrate learning. Computer applications for drawing sketches and illustrations also have become commonplace, and often are integrated into word processing software found on most classroom computers. Students who have limited ability to write or use a keyboard can use these applications in lieu of other means of expression.

Oral Presentation

Oral presentations are commonly used in some classrooms, but teachers may not view them as alternatives to traditional written means of expression. Students who may not be able to write can present information orally to the entire class, in small groups, or one-on-one. Oral presentations can be made more effective when the teacher structures the task for students who may need assistance organizing ideas. Also, use of other materials in conjunction with an oral presentation can simplify the process. For example, rather than writing a paragraph, a student could create a poster and then describe it. Of course, the computer software described above also could be helpful here.

Models and Manipulatives

It is often possible to structure tasks and activities so that students can construct models or use simple manipulatives to express ideas or communicate learning. Familiar examples of this strategy include use of Styrofoam balls and toothpicks to build a model of a molecule, or creation of a model of the solar system using strings and balls. However, there are many other ways for students to express themselves using simple manipulatives. Not only does this strategy allow students who have limited means of expression to communicate, but it also can support knowledge transfer and development of abstract or analogical reasoning, particularly when simple, readily available manipulatives are used.

FLEXIBLE MEANS OF ENGAGEMENT

As we have emphasized throughout this book, access to the general curriculum implies that all children have the opportunity to learn challenging content. It is likely that most teachers would agree with the philosophy of this premise when the "all" includes students who have sensory or motor deficits that interfere with access to the curriculum. Most teachers also would support this assertion when the "all" includes students from diverse racial, ethnic, language, or cultural groups. What is troublesome for many teachers, though, is the idea of accommodating students who have learning or cognitive disabilities so that they may access the same curriculum as all other students. For many teachers, accommodating these students often is interpreted as watering down the curriculum and can be viewed as somehow being unfair to the other students in the class who manage to achieve on their own.

However, when there are multiple ways for students to be engaged in the general education curriculum, it is possible for students of differing abilities and backgrounds to be comparably challenged by the same content. One way to accomplish this goal is through attention to the format of the information you are teaching (i.e., facts, concepts, principles, or procedures). Knowing what kind of information you are teaching can help you decide (a) how to teach it and (b) what students should do with it. This focus can also help the teacher remove extraneous information or requirements, such as unnecessary vocabulary or confusing graphics, from the information.

Recall that in the last chapter, we talked about the various cognitive processes learners use to learn and remember different kinds of information and the different kinds of intellectual activities that can be performed with various kinds of information. Students of differing abilities can be comparably challenged by the same content by performing different cognitive operations. For example, in a middle school science class, some students can illustrate the concept "erosion" by selecting, from among several examples, the one that best shows the concept. At the same time, others in the class might be asked to evaluate two events and report which is a better example of erosion and why.

Similarly, the instruction might provide different points of access for the same information. For example, a geography lesson about state government might include the following goals for different members of the class:

Name our state capital (reiterate a fact).

Give an example of a state capital (illustrate a concept).

Tell the difference between a county and a state (evaluate a concept).

Tell why states have capitals (apply a principle).

It is essential however, for teachers to have a clear understanding of what precisely they are intending to teach. For example, if the goal is to teach the concept of erosion, then none of the instructional techniques just described will give an unfair advantage to any one student; rather, the techniques, used in combination, simply ensure that all students have access to the concept. In contrast, if the goals of the lesson include enhancing the ability to write about technical concepts, then the teacher may need to consider how to provide accommodations for individual students in the concept and provide directed instruction in writing.

ACCOMMODATIONS

An accommodation typically is defined as a service or support that is provided to help a student fully access the subject matter and instruction; it also validly demonstrates what the student knows. An accommodation changes neither the grade-level instructional content nor the achievement expectations. Accommodations should not interfere with, or substantively change, the content standards including the facts, knowledge, and underlying constructs specified for students. In addition, accommodations mean that a student with a disability is expected to learn, to the same defined level of proficiency, all of the content that "typical" students at the student's grade level will learn. The gray band in Figure 5.3 shows where, on the continuum of curriculum access, an education that includes accommodations would fall. Notice in the figure that the educational program still consists primarily of work in the general curriculum but that a substantial portion of the student's program involves special education or related services that may be largely designed to support the student's access to, and progress in, the general education curriculum.

It is important to remember that IEP planning must attend to accommodations in the areas related to a student's disability across the **entire** general education curriculum. That is, if a student has a reading disability, teachers must plan for how they will accommodate or support the student's reading in all subject matter content that requires reading, including math, science, art, physical education, and so on, without altering the curricular goals or expected student learning outcomes.

Accommodations can be as simple as pencil grips, large print books, or a quieter place for the student to learn. More marked accommodations might include allowing a student more time to complete an assignment or test, allowing calculators or spell checkers, or allowing students to use simple word

Figure 5.3 Curriculum Access Continuum

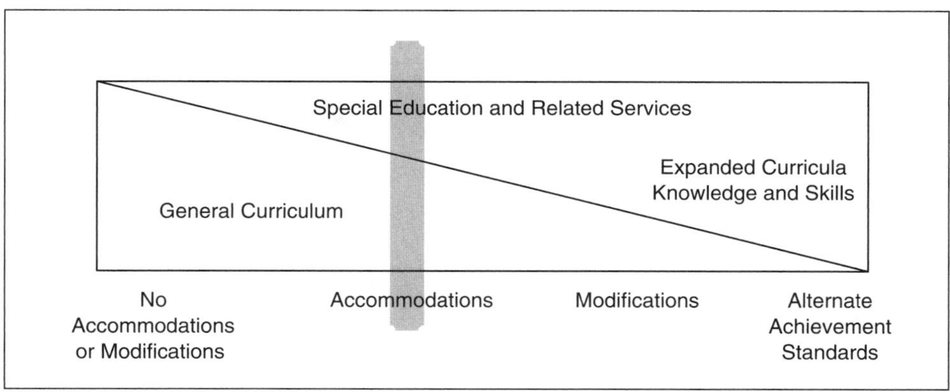

processing software for written assignments. Accommodations also can include providing more practice of specific skills, more opportunities for applying skills or concepts, and direct instruction in using specific knowledge in different contexts. In fact, increasing a student's opportunity to learn by increasing the time allocated to instruction and providing specific instructional strategies may be among the most powerful accommodations teachers can make.

Deciding on accommodations requires that teachers have a sound knowledge of the key constructs—the facts, skills, and concepts—embedded in a specific lesson or instructional unit. Teachers must understand that the accommodation does not alter the big idea or major learning outcomes expected of the instruction and requires teachers to have a deep understanding of the content domain. In general, accommodations fall into three categories: alternative acquisition modes, content enhancements, and alternative response modes.

Alternative Acquisition Modes

The purpose of alternative acquisition strategies is to augment, bypass, or compensate for a motor-, sensory-, or information-processing deficit (Lewis, 1993). Decisions to provide these kinds of accommodations most likely will involve a multidisciplinary team that includes therapists (occupational, physical, speech) or other specialists with expertise in adaptive technology. A complete discussion of the range of adaptive supports available for students who have motor, sensory, or cognitive deficits is beyond the scope of this book; however, it is likely that most teachers are familiar with alternative acquisition tools of one form or another. These accommodations can include sign language interpreters, Braille materials, voice-output computers, and tape-recorded books.

Content Enhancements

Students who have learning problems often need assistance managing the strategic aspects of learning, and content enhancements can help in this area. Content enhancements, as described by Lenz, Bulgren, and Hudson (1990), are techniques that help students identify, organize, comprehend, and remember content information. Content enhancements can include a number of supports with which many teachers already are familiar, including the following examples (Hudson, Lignugaris-Kraft, & Miller, 1993).

Advance Organizers. These are preinstructional materials designed to enhance students' linkage of new information with prior knowledge stored in long-term memory. Advance organizers may be verbal or written, and they may be presented in question format. Examples include questions presented prior to a discussion or reading assignment, vocabulary words presented on the board or a handout, or verbal statements presented by the teacher and designed to activate prior knowledge prior to instruction.

Visual Displays. These include diagrams, concrete models, videos, or digital material designed to portray the relationships among various pieces of information presented during instruction. Visual displays are intended to help students organize information in long-term memory and activate prior knowledge during instruction. They function as an accommodation to the extent that they scaffold the creation of networks of information in the learner's long-term memory. Additional examples include graphic organizers, concept maps, and video segments intended to anchor or situate the student's learning in a meaningful context.

Study Guides. These are worksheets that are provided to the student prior to a reading or study assignment that include a set of statements or questions intended to focus the student's attention and cognitive resources on the key information to be learned. Study guides can take the form of completed or partially completed outlines; questions focusing on the textual, literal, and inferential aspects of a study assignment; or various other tasks designed to prompt active processing of the material to be studied.

Mnemonic Devices. Techniques to assist in the storage and recall of declarative knowledge associated with content domains, mnemonics may be verbal or pictorial and may be provided by the teacher or developed collaboratively by the teacher and the student. Most teachers are familiar with some of the common examples of mnemonics, such as use of key words, pictures, or symbols. ROY G BIV and Every Good Boy Deserved Fudge are classic mnemonic devices.

Peer-Mediated Instruction. This form of content enhancement employs peers as instructional agents within the classroom. It can take the form of peer and cross-age tutoring, classwide tutoring, or cooperative learning. The primary purpose of peer-mediated instruction is to increase the number of opportunities for distributed practice with feedback. This approach usually entails fairly well-scripted or structured interactions designed and mediated by the teacher.

Alternative Response Modes

Expression serves a number of functions for students beyond simply answering teacher questions and making needs known. Formulating and expressing ideas is an integral part of the learning and assessment process. Therefore, it is important to find multiple ways for all students to express themselves to reduce barriers created by sensory or motor deficits, or language differences. Of course, the way students most often communicate in classrooms is through speaking and writing, so whenever acceptable alternatives to those modes of expression can be employed, curriculum access is increased.

An example of a more specialized alternative response mode is use of a scribe to transcribe a student's responses, for example, to test items. An instructional assistant (rather than another student) often serves in this role to ensure accurate verbatim recording of the student's thoughts. Untimed response situations also can sometimes be used as an accommodation for students who need more time to complete work.

MODIFICATIONS

When a curriculum modification is made, either the specific subject matter is altered, or the performance level expected of students is changed. A curriculum modification is made when a student is either taught something different from the rest of the class or taught the same information but at a different level of complexity. For example, the rest of the class may be expected to tell the distinguishing characteristics of animal and plant cells, but a student for whom a modification has been made may be required to discriminate between animals and plants, given pictures and short descriptions.

The decision to make an instructional modification is an important one and should not be made lightly; neither should it be made by one teacher acting alone. Modifications require a team decision. There are both long- and short-term implications of curricular modifications. For example, some modifications may put the student at a great disadvantage on assessments, and those assessments may have significant consequences for students as well as for schools. Keep in mind, however, that a curriculum modification does not equate to a change in the setting where a student is educated. Modifications to curriculum can and should be provided in the general education classroom unless the IEP can clearly justify why this will not occur.

The gray line in Figure 5.4 shows where, on the continuum of curriculum access, a program that includes modifications would fall. Notice that at this point, a large part of the program involves special education and related services depending on the student's need for specialized modifications and support services.

A common modification frequently offered to students receiving special education is to reduce an assignment by giving fewer problems or asking students to write one or two paragraphs instead of a report of several pages. Often teachers believe that reducing an assignment is a simple "accommodation." However, these types of modifications can "water down" the curriculum by taking away the difficult tasks and altering what students are expected to learn. In effect, these types of modifications can reduce a student's opportunity to learn the critical knowledge, skills, and concepts related to a particular

Figure 5.4 Curriculum Access Continuum

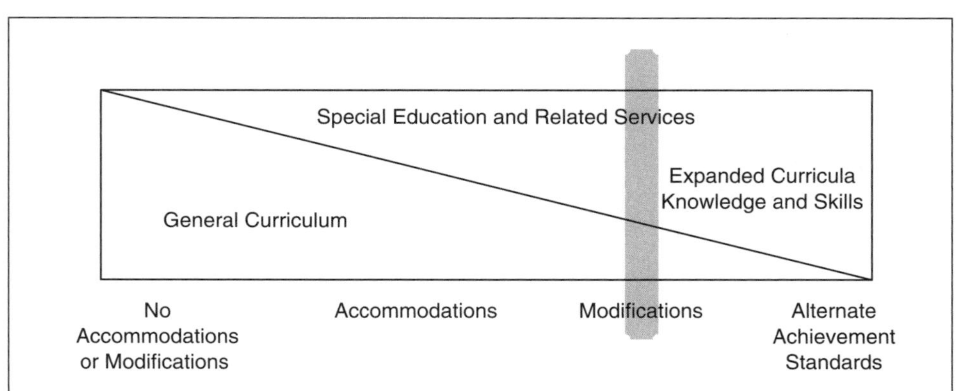

subject. Modifications must be made within the context of the content and achievement standards that are the foundation of the curriculum. We will discuss this further in the next chapter when we address setting IEP goals.

Modifying what a student learns moves further along the continuum of curriculum access. A modification may begin by keeping the subject matter and essential curricular goals and objectives the same but changing the materials used in the lesson, such as providing lower level reading material. For example, some students in a language arts class may be reading literature at different reading levels, but all are working on identifying character development, plot, and voice.

More significant modifications occur as a teacher designs new material and tasks for individual children that mirror the general education curriculum in the broadest sense (e.g., all of the students are receiving math instruction, but the difficulty ranges from basic algebra to solving simple computation problems using a calculator or "survival mathematics"). A similar level of modification would be using a textbook that covers the same subject matter but is written in language that is below the grade level of the class. That is, some students may use a science textbook or science materials that are one or more grade levels below their peers. While this strategy may reduce reading demands, they also do not provide an opportunity to learn important grade-level concepts, vocabulary, and other key skills.

The possible implications of making modifications may be significant when curriculum variables discussed in Chapter 2 are considered. For example, it would be important to ensure that use of off-grade-level material does not interfere with the curriculum sequencing strategy and later result in the student having even greater gaps in knowledge than might otherwise be created by the student's learning deficit alone. Simply modifying curricular materials because of a student's reading level may not be the best decision. Rather, providing accommodations and supports, no matter how extensive, that permit the student to learn the grade-level concepts and vocabulary is a far better alternative.

Teaching Less Content

Teaching less content implies that there is some information that a student can "get by" without learning. Frequently, teachers make this modification to help students keep up with classmates as they progress through segments of the curriculum. The assumption is that reducing content will bypass the student's learning problems. However, just because you find that a student cannot keep pace with the general education curriculum or learn at the same rate as most of the other students in the class, this is not always a good reason for making reductions to what a student will have a chance to learn or be held accountable for. Again, before reducing what a student learns, considerations for accommodations, such as more practice sessions or more intensive instruction, should be made.

Teaching Different Content

Teaching different content implies that the expected general education curriculum is different for a particular student than for the rest of the class. The primary reason for making this modification is to provide instruction in content deemed important for the student, that is, content that will not be taught in the general education curriculum. For example, a student who needs more explicit instruction in functional skills, such as how to make a schedule or learn to access transportation, may have IEP goals and instruction that are very different from the general education curriculum and instruction. However, sometimes teaching such functional skills or content can be achieved by enhancing, not altering or substituting, what is taught in the general education classroom.

Individualized Curriculum Goals

Finally, at the most extreme end of the curriculum continuum are students whose curricular goals, while linked to the general education content standards, may be in areas that are clearly highly individualized (e.g., communication and social awareness). The gray band in Figure 5.5 refers to these students. These small numbers of students work in a highly differentiated or expanded general education curriculum. For them, access is defined more in terms of participation in curricular activities than in terms of receiving the same information or concepts as their same age peers. Keep in mind, however, that NCLB requires that there be only one set of content standards that apply to all students, including those with the most significant cognitive disabilities. Thus, even a highly individualized set of learning goals will need to be referenced to a state's content standards.

ACCOMMODATIONS, MODIFICATIONS, AND ASSESSMENT

When teachers modify the curriculum for students with disabilities, they alter the link between instruction and assessment. Teachers need to be very aware of what knowledge and skills are being assessed, so that when they make

Figure 5.5 Curriculum Access Continuum

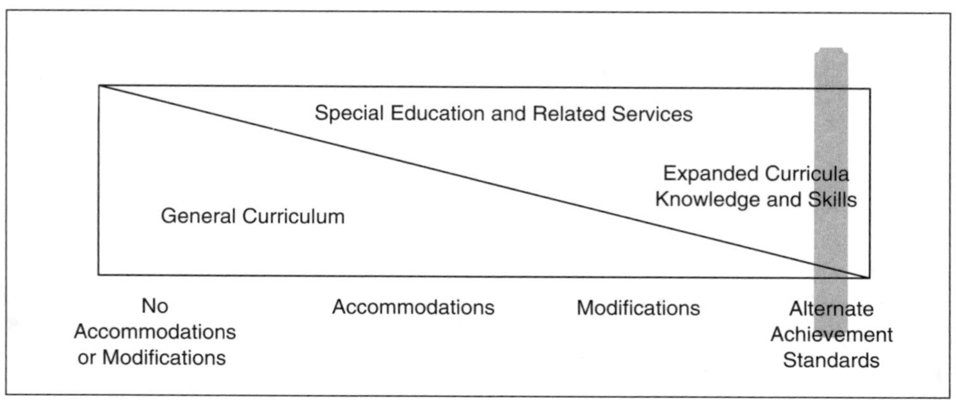

modifications, they maintain the essential constructs that students will need to demonstrate in the state or district assessment.

Decisions to accommodate or modify curricula have implications for how students will participate in state and district assessments. For example, if a student can fully access specific general education content without instructional accommodation, that student should take whatever assessments are required in that subject matter without accommodations. Similarly, if a student receives an accommodation during instruction in a specific subject matter, the same accommodation should be provided during assessment. Some standardized assessments currently being administered in school districts permit only certain accommodations and restrict the use of all accommodations that may be provided during instruction.

For those few students who may have very individualized learning goals, the use of an alternate assessment to the state or district assessment is the most appropriate and valid way to measure achievement.

SPECIAL EDUCATION AND RELATED SERVICES

For every student with an IEP, there is an expectation that special education and related services will be provided to meet that student's unique needs. The decisions to provide related services may not impact decisions regarding a student's access to the general curriculum, or they may serve as important accommodations. For students who receive speech therapy to correct articulation or fluency difficulties, curriculum access may not be an issue. Others may require specialized therapies that help them with writing or other motor functions and accommodate and support instruction. Intensive, related service goals for students with the most significant disabilities become part of a very different curriculum. Assistive technology, transition services, and the specialized supports provided to students with visual or hearing impairments are parts of the mix of individual services and supports to be considered during IEP planning.

Special education interventions refer to the full array of instructional assessments, strategies, accommodations, and supports that are offered to help a student meet IEP goals. Special education and related services may occur within or outside of the general education classroom and are not influenced by the degree to which a student is accessing the general education curriculum. In other words, students who may be pursuing all or most of the general education curricular goals may need as much or as intensive special education services as students with very different curricular goals.

The intent of the IEP is that the student will receive an individualized assessment of educational performance that will lead to individualized goals, objectives, and instruction; these goals, however, must be based on the general curriculum. Individualizing goals, objectives, and instruction within the context of providing access to the general education curriculum is among the more difficult tasks that IEP teams now face. In the next chapter, we present a decision process for developing IEPs. Key questions and examples are presented to help the IEP team engage in individual planning for special education students.

6 A Decision-Making Process for Creating IEPs That Lead to Curriculum Access

By now, you should be acquainted with how to find the general education curriculum and how to assess a student's performance within that curriculum. You should also be able to distinguish between a curriculum accommodation and a curriculum modification, as well as an alternate assessment and alternate achievement standards, and how to design instruction that matches the type of content you must teach. Now we need to discuss how to consolidate all of these pieces to create an individualized education program (IEP) for a specific student with a disability.

In Chapter 1, we described the required components of an IEP that directly relate to accessing the general education curriculum and participating in state and district assessments. Those are only some of what is required to be addressed in an IEP.

Now we discuss how to proceed with a planning process that links IEP goals to standards. The process we outline does not address every aspect of what IEP planning should involve, nor should it be confused with an actual IEP document. All school districts have established their own forms and procedures for developing IEPs, which reflect the requirements in the 2004 Individuals with Disabilities Education Improvement Act (New IDEA). Our process gives IEP teams a logical and sequential way to think about an individual student in relation to a standards-based curriculum. First, we will describe the essential decision points in IEP planning, and then we will apply these to some individual students.

Figure 6.1 provides a flow chart to help guide you through the key decisions that the IEP team must make as they think about how to ensure that a student with a disability accesses the general education curriculum. It might be helpful to compare an actual IEP form with which you are familiar to our process as we discuss each step.

Figure 6.1 An IEP Decision-Making Process

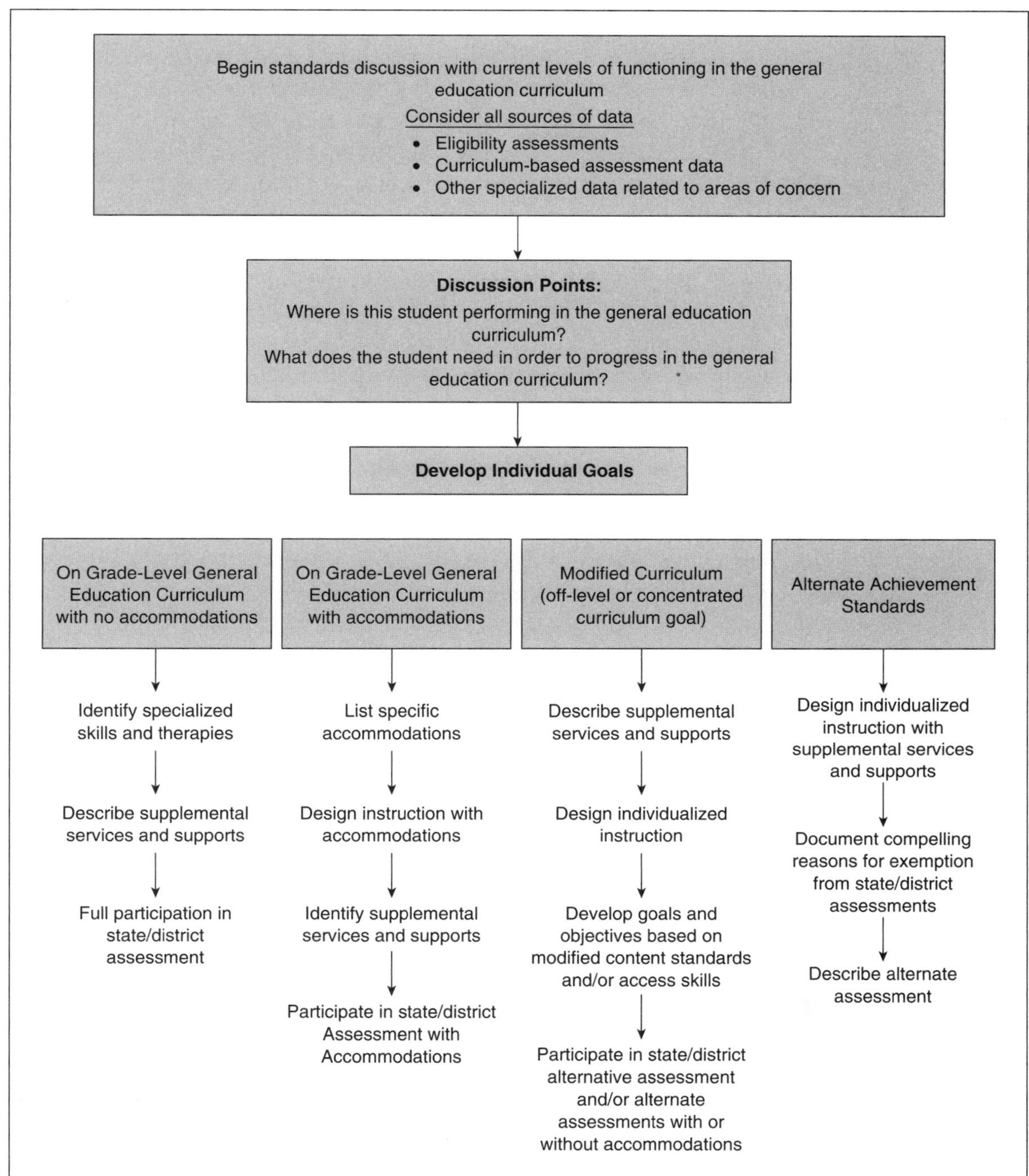

STEP 1: INSTRUCTIONAL ASSESSMENT

The IEP process begins with an analysis of a student's present levels of academic achievement and functional performance, including how the disability affects the student's involvement and progress in the general education curriculum.

The assessment strategies we discussed in Chapter 4 will be critical in this analysis. Please note, though, that as we consider assessment here, we are assuming that evaluation to determine eligibility already has occurred and that the adverse educational impact of the student's disability has been identified.

This first step toward access requires the IEP planning team to define the student's current level of academic achievement and functional performance in *all* of the curricular areas that may be affected by the disability. Instructional assessment at this stage involves collecting information about levels of performance in each of the subject matter areas addressed in the general education curriculum. Assessment of specific skills and operations is also required. This analysis will have to include more than a simple inventory of skills, such as math computations or a reading comprehension score, obtained from an off-the-shelf assessment instrument. Instructional assessment for IEP planning must be referenced to local general education curriculum goals that are aligned with state content and achievement standards. Assessments must focus on the content and organization of the student's information networks, a topic discussed in Chapter 3. The team has to understand what underlying knowledge and learning strategies a student has acquired through prior learning and experience and how well the student applies that information to a variety of contexts. Remember: Do not fall into the trap of thinking that because a student has not mastered a basic skill such as reading decoding, he or she is not ready to understand more complex knowledge or operations.

Knowledge of the general education curriculum is essential to the IEP decision-making process and is the primary reason that the IEP team must include someone who has that curricular knowledge. However, special education teachers and other service providers also need to understand the scope of content and sequence of the curriculum. The decision framework for finding the general curriculum, presented at the end of Chapter 2, will help team members identify the knowledge, skills, and processes that will need to be assessed. This will require a three-phase process:

Phase 1: Identify the critical, enduring knowledge associated with the general education curriculum within each subject matter domain that all students at a particular grade level are expected to learn.

Phase 2: Analyze the key knowledge, skills, and processes that a skilled learner must have to be proficient in using that core knowledge. This step is somewhat analogous to the process of task analysis familiar to many special educators, except that it is not hierarchical (e.g., moving downward to the lowest possible level of skill) and it does not involve the kind of fine-grained molecular analysis that often results in irrelevant goals and objectives focused on meaningless subcomponents of basic skills. Remember that the whole is bigger than the sum of the parts when we are talking about the kind of generative thinking and problem solving that is required in the general education curriculum.

Keep in mind the core elements of curriculum that we discussed in Chapter 2: Curriculum has a purpose, it involves a domain, and it involves time. Think about the overall goals that the math, science, or language arts curriculum is intended to accomplish. Examine the goals for a specific grade level or range. Look back to see what these curriculum goals expect students to have already learned, and look ahead to see what the students will be expected to learn in the near and far future. Finally, consider how the various types of facts, concepts, rules, and processes fit together in the curriculum to help the student develop more expert knowledge networks.

Phase 3: Determine the individual student's use of the critical knowledge, skills, and learning processes and strategies, as we discussed in Chapter 3. For example, you will want to have information about the student's skill level in areas such as basic reading, more specifically, phonemic analysis, fluency, specific vocabulary, and language structures and concepts. In fact, in each subject matter area, you need to know more than just a student's test results. You need to understand if low performance is due to problems with retention and learning processes or if it may be related to the ways in which a student is expected to demonstrate knowledge. For example, are the student's difficulties with written expression preventing the student from demonstrating the depth of knowledge of a specific topic?

Assessment must also include how the student accesses information to solve problems and learn new things. For example, think about how a student's learning and memory problems might interfere with accessing and using strategic knowledge about reading. If students fail to activate a comprehension strategy such as multipass, is it because (a) they never learned the strategy in the first place, (b) they forgot how to initiate the strategy, or (c) they don't recognize the features in a reading task that would indicate that the strategy would be helpful? The type of specialized instruction indicated on an IEP will be somewhat different under each of these conditions.

Of course, you will also want to know what past instructional strategies have worked to help this student learn. This analysis will involve some of the assessment tools discussed in Chapter 4 as well as a more general analysis of the learning processes involved in acquisition and use of the information to be learned, presented in Chapter 3.

The following questions can guide your assessment:

- **What will "typical" students at this child's grade level be expected to know and to do in the subject matter curriculum (math, science, reading, physical education, etc.) during the time frame addressed by the IEP (typically one school year)?**
- **What are the key goals or performance expectations associated with the subject matter knowledge?** Define precisely what a proficient level of student achievement looks like. Examples include being able to (a) read independently specific types of text and answer certain types of questions, (b) accurately estimate size and measures in a variety of daily situations, and (c) write a coherent multiparagraph, persuasive essay that logically develops an idea and conforms to rules of grammar and punctuation.
- **How is the target student currently performing in these areas?** Look at a variety of evidence, including curriculum-based assessments, work samples, and input from parents, teachers, and other IEP team members. The criterion-referenced assessment strategies we discussed in Chapter 4 would be useful here. Also useful is examining work samples

of other students who are considered to be proficient or advanced as well as students at or below basics in the specific grade-level subject matter. Teachers can determine what the performance targets are and also identify the areas in which a specific student needs additional instruction.

- **In what ways are the student's disabilities impacting his or her performance?** In addition to specific skill deficits, such as in reading or math, educational assessments should consider such things as the student's focus on, and attention to, instruction; the student's organizational skills; and other learning processes. Information in Chapter 3 may be helpful here.

The outcome of Step 1 of the IEP decision-making process is a clearly defined road map that defines a student's starting point with respect to grade-level standards and curriculum goals in various subject areas in addition to the learning that must be developed.

STEP 2: CHOOSING IEP GOALS AND IDENTIFYING SUPPORTS

At this step in the process, you have accumulated a body of evidence that identifies the student's level of performance in the curriculum. Is there evidence that the student requires additional intensive instruction to attain proficiency or make progress in particular areas of the curriculum? If so, what accommodations, modifications, and specialized instruction or other services does the student require within the specific curriculum area? In other words, what does the student need to catch up or keep up?

For example, a sixth-grade student may have a basic understanding of grade-level scientific concepts and terminology, but ability to read the science textbook is below grade level. This student will require more intensive vocabulary drills and reading accommodations in order to keep up in the science area. He may also need direct instruction in reading fluency and basic writing processes *and* require accommodations (such as a writing software program and a spell checker) to help him in the general education curriculum. This student's IEP must include goals to improve academic achievement and functional performance in specific skill areas. It also must address how the student will be supported and accommodated in other areas in order to continue to progress in the grade-level curriculum. The examples in Box 6.1 and Box 6.2 illustrate the process of selecting an IEP goal and identifying appropriate supports.

Boxes 6.1 and 6.2 illustrate two examples of curricular accommodations. In Jason's case, he can be expected to fully access the grade-level standards with accommodations. In Felix's case, he will access grade-level content and achievement expectations, with accommodations, in core areas of the curriculum and will also have curriculum modifications in other areas. In both cases, we would expect these students to be able to fully access and progress in the general education curriculum and make progress toward meeting achievement standards.

Now you are ready to actually create IEP goals, objectives, and benchmarks.

Box 6.1 Jason

Jason is a seventh grader who has been receiving special education services since fourth grade. He is a struggling reader and has difficulty with his writing and spelling. Jason is a very slow reader, and as a result, he struggles to complete assignments and his comprehension suffers. However, he has reasonable understanding of material presented orally and is able to complete in-class work when teachers make effective use of the principles of universal design for learning and when there are additional cues available in the environment, such as diagrams on the overhead projector, step-by step directions on the white board, or graphic organizers and study guide worksheets.

When the teachers examined the requirements for each of the core academic areas, they confirmed that Jason is not a fluent reader and often needs help reading textbooks and other curriculum materials. They also noticed that he has specific gaps in the writing process and has both spelling and vocabulary deficits.

Jason's IEP team determines that there are two areas that need to be addressed. First, the IEP team needs to specify the types of accommodations and instructional supports that will help Jason compensate for his slow reading in the content areas. They will also specify strategies for helping him organize his learning process. The overall goal is to help Jason begin to develop well-organized, accessible knowledge networks in various subject matter domains. This will help him learn more complex information later in the curriculum. What will be most important is that he will need to have information represented in multiple formats. Accommodations could include structured study guides, peer study-buddies, and frequent opportunities to use content information in hands-on activities that require complex problem solving but do not require extensive reading.

Second, Jason needs intensive support in reading and writing. The IEP team determines that the special education teacher and reading specialist will implement a specific reading program to help him develop word attack skills. The teacher will also begin intensive drills to strengthen Jason's vocabulary in specific subject areas. The vocabulary list will be developed in collaboration with Jason's content area teachers and will focus on the essential terminology in each area. The special education teacher also will need to help the student acquire, and access readily, a broad repertoire of comprehension strategies that can be employed to learn content area information. A specific writing program will also be initiated to help Jason strengthen his writing processes. These areas require measurable annual goals.

STEP 3: CREATING IEP ANNUAL GOALS

IEP annual goals are the targets that individual students need to reach by the end of an instructional year. Note that the 2004 amendments to IDEA did not

Box 6.2 Felix

Felix, a third grader, has been identified as having both attention deficit hyperactivity disorder and a communication disorder. Felix is not yet reading independently, although he does know his alphabet and most of the letter-sound relationships. While he does not have difficulty speaking, his verbal and written language is developmentally far below that of his peers. Felix also has difficulty paying attention through a typical lesson, and teachers report that "he seems to drift off during class and is very forgetful."

An evaluation of Felix indicates that he has a slightly below average IQ but has some areas (e.g., general knowledge and spatial reasoning) where he is at or above age-level norms.

Felix needs to be given access to the fourth-grade standards and curriculum. He must also be given specific reading instruction as well as instruction in spelling, writing, and language development. This is a tall order, and Felix's special and general education teachers must make some hard decisions that will require a good understanding of the general education standards.

First, it is clear that Felix's IEP goals must address basic reading literacy as well as language development skills (e.g., increase vocabulary and develop more complex sentence structures). His teachers know that Felix needs accommodations and supports to help him learn the fourth-grade content, but given his attention difficulties and his poor language functioning, they know that learning will be slower for him and that he will not be able to keep pace with the entire fourth-grade curriculum.

In math, his teachers determine that Felix needs remediation in the area of computation, but that he will use a calculator and a writing software program during lessons involving problem solving and math applications. They also agree to focus only on the most important or essential curriculum objectives within math.

For example, the fourth-grade math standards for expressions, equations, and inequalities address the following objectives:

(a) Write and identify expressions.
(b) Represent numeric quantities using operational symbols (+, −, ×, ÷ with no remainders).
(c) Determine equivalent expressions and identify, write, solve, and apply equations and inequalities.
(d) Represent relationships using relational symbols (>, <, =) and operational symbols (+, −, ×, ÷) on either side.
(e) Use operational symbols (+, −, ×) and whole numbers (0–200).
(f) Find the unknown in an equation with one operation.

Felix's math and special education teachers collaboratively determine that Felix needs to know the concept of equivalent values and also the basic procedures for creating equivalency. He also needs to understand the operational symbols, so they identify a core set of 20 terms that they consider

(Continued)

Box 6.2 (Continued)

crucial to meet this standard. They discuss the materials that might be used to teach the concepts and agree that they will focus first on one- and two-digit whole numbers.

Similar decisions are made for science and social studies; Felix will have access to computer-based curriculum materials to help him acquire science and social studies information. In addition, the special education teacher designs some simple strategies (such as those discussed in Chapter 3) to help Felix focus on the main idea and develop a sequence for how to approach new learning tasks.

In the reading and language arts area, Felix will devote most of his time to increasing basic word attack skills and fluency. However, he will also keep abreast of other key curriculum standards, such as developing and applying vocabulary through exposure to a variety of texts including listening to, independently reading, and discussing a variety of literary and informational texts. Some specific support strategies his teachers will employ include:

- Discussing words and word meanings daily as they are encountered in texts, instruction, and conversation
- Identifying 12 to 20 new words for deeper study each week and developing a conceptual understanding of new words
- Selecting a number of grade-level books on tape as well as other literature at Felix's reading level
- Selecting vocabulary words from subject matter content and allowing him to select words from books at his reading level.

include the requirement that IEPs state objectives or benchmarks, except in the case of those very few students who will take alternate assessments aligned to alternate achievement standards. For these students, the IEP team must specify annual goals and objectives or benchmarks. IEP goals should be clear enough to focus instruction and be able to be measured and reported on periodically. At the same time, goals should not be so microscopic that they limit what is taught. Goals should clearly reflect the general education content and achievement standards and curriculum.

For those students whose IEPs require either instructional objectives or benchmarks, these are simply more discrete stops toward the eventual target or annual goal, perhaps linked to grading periods or other natural breaks in an academic calendar. The parts of an instructional objective are described in Box 6.3. If you need more information about how to develop effective instructional objectives, a tried and true reference is Robert F. Mager's (1997) *Preparing Instructional Objectives: A Critical Tool in the Development of Effective Instruction.*

Box 6.3 Anatomy of an Instructional Objective

The terms "goal" and "objective" often are used interchangeably. Goals indicate the long-term outcomes expected to result from instruction, and objectives are the interim steps along the way. In the IEP, goals usually have an annual focus, and objectives generally reflect what is expected to occur in the next quarter. Content and performance standards in state and district curriculum frameworks can be thought of as goals that have a 1- to 3-year focus. Regardless of their time focus, all goals and objectives answer the following questions:

Who?	Will do?	What?	How well?	Under what conditions?

Who?	Specifies who will be expected to accomplish the goal.
Will do?	An action verb that can be observed when executed.
What?	Tells *specifically* what the student will do.
How well?	Specifies the minimum standard you establish for accomplishing the goal. If this standard is not met, the goal has not been accomplished.
Under what conditions?	Indicates the context in which the goal will be observed. This is an indication of the "level of difficulty." For example, "in 3 minutes on a test" represents a very different set of conditions than "overnight for homework."

Here is an example of a quarterly objective you might develop for a student learning to incorporate peer feedback into a final essay draft:

Who?	*Will do?*	*What?*	*How well?*	*Under what conditions?*
Roger	will write	a final version of a creative essay	with no spelling or punctuation errors	after his writing partner has proofread his first draft.

Instructional objectives originally were championed by educators working in the behaviorist tradition. This has led some teachers to believe that instructional objectives are not appropriate for dimensions such as student

(Continued)

Box 6.3 (Continued)

attitudes or thinking skills that cannot be readily observed. While it is true that not all important educational outcomes can be measured directly, objectives *can* be written for affective or covert cognitive operations. To do so, think about how you would know your instruction has been effective and the desired change in thinking has occurred. For example, suppose you want your student to develop an appreciation for various genres of writing (e.g., essay, biography, science fiction, romance, etc.). Here is a quarterly objective you might write:

During the next two months . . .

Who?	*Will do?*	*What?*	*How well?*	*Under what conditions?*
Diane	will select	at least three different types	of reading	when given a choice during free time.

When developing IEPs that are referenced to the general education curriculum, teachers should think about setting annual goals that incorporate what students in general education are expected to learn during a particular time period (e.g., during a semester, an academic year, an instructional unit, a grading period, or a multi-year span of time (e.g., Grades K–3, 6–8, etc.) that represents a major transition point in the curriculum.

Thinking about the multiyear goals is important for several reasons. First, special education teachers must keep their eye on what all students are expected to know and demonstrate on the key state and local assessments each year; these assessments reflect accumulated knowledge. This is particularly important when the results of those assessments have consequences for individual students, such as determining whether they are promoted to another grade or receive a high school diploma. Individual students' IEPs should represent stepping stones toward more advanced levels of the curriculum. Teachers cannot afford to set goals that reflect very fragmented or discrete learner expectations for a limited time period, such as one year. While these have traditionally been the types of goals written for IEPs, they will not move the student forward toward the larger sets of knowledge, skills, and processes defined by state standards and measured by state and district assessments.

The Challenge

Past practices in IEP development frequently have focused on measuring the discrete skill deficits of a student with a disability and then task analyzing the skills to identify the smallest teachable units. The specific skill deficits frequently became the annual IEP goals, and the smallest teachable units were translated into IEP objectives. These practices were based on assumptions that learning was hierarchical and that learning more complex skills could not occur until a student mastered all of the small units. This approach will not work for the type of learning we now expect of students. Nor will this approach to defining IEP goals (and objectives or benchmarks) match the type of instruction that is expected of teachers if students are to access the general education curriculum. The following questions will help you translate the knowledge about where a student is functioning in the curriculum into actual IEP goals.

Do We Need a Goal?

In our IEP decision-making process, annual goals and objectives or benchmarks are defined only in those subject matter or educational need areas where a general education curricular goal or content standard is modified or an alternate achievement standard is specified for a student. That is, if a student is expected to demonstrate the same level of achievement of the same knowledge and skills as the student's general education grade-level peers, with or without accommodations, no IEP goals should be required. However, the curricular and instructional supports and accommodations, and the individuals responsible for providing those supports, must be clearly described in the IEP.

Individualized IEP goals should be specified for related services as well as in areas of educational need that may be outside of the general curriculum where the student may be receiving specialized instruction. For example, goals related to speech and language, occupational therapy, or physical therapy may be specified. In addition, social and behavioral goals and supports, specific learning strategies that may be taught, or other skills that are outside of the general curriculum need to be addressed in IEP goals.

The other important questions you will need to answer are:

- **What do we expect the student to be able to do at the end of this instructional year in the areas we identified?**
- **Do we expect the student to be able to demonstrate the same level of achievement or performance in the same manner as a typical student?**
- **Will the student need accommodations? If so, which ones and in which subjects? Will these accommodations also be required during assessments?**

Review the discussion of accommodations in Chapter 5 regarding their purpose as well as the potential types of activities or supports that may be considered accommodations. For example, additional instruction may be provided, or special instruction may substitute for classroom instruction. A student may receive reading instruction through an approach more explicit than that used with other students in the class. There may also be additional opportunities for re-teaching, using more representations, and for practice.

Before considering modifying specific general education curriculum goals, the IEP team should consider if all possible accommodations to the general education curriculum have been made.

Setting IEP Goals for Curriculum Modifications and Alternate Achievement Standards

If the IEP team determines that some part of the general education curriculum must be modified or alternate achievement standards established for a student, the first step is to review whether the student has had access to all possible instructional accommodations and to specifically identify the discrete areas of specific subject matter, knowledge, skills, and processes that may require modifications. IEP goals need to be specified in those areas, and both general and special educators and parents must consult and collaborate on decisions to modify the general education curriculum. Decisions to modify should not be made lightly, because once a student is moved away from the general education curriculum, it is unlikely to expect the student to return to grade-level performance. All members of the IEP team must carefully consider how the changes in content reduce the student's opportunity to learn important knowledge and how that lack of opportunity may impact later achievement and educational outcomes.

Developing annual IEP goals that reflect a modified curriculum require what we earlier referred to as "educational triage" wherein the teachers must decide on the key or critical knowledge within a specific content domain. Questions important to making this determination include:

Will We Teach the Same Content but Define an Alternate Achievement Expectation?

Here, the decision is to expose the student to all of the same knowledge and basic concepts that are provided to the typical student but reduce or alter the expectations of what the student will have to achieve or be able to demonstrate. This decision is very much related to teaching less content; it assumes that although the student will receive instruction in all of what is taught, the student is expected to learn less or at a lower level than the typical same-age peer.

This is a very tricky modification because it assumes that instructional time and other resources will be devoted to fitting the student into all of the classroom instruction, even though the student will have alternate expectations. However, IEP teams are at risk of making ad hoc decisions about what to leave in and what to omit in the general education curriculum that could result in the student losing opportunities to learn important material or specific skills that address other critical educational needs beyond the general education curriculum.

Will We Teach Less Content?

Reducing the overall amount of subject matter content that a student will be explicitly taught is different from teaching the same content but changing the performance expectations. There are a variety of ways to make this modification: The student achieves fewer objectives or curricular benchmarks, the student completes shorter units or parts of a unit, the student reads fewer pages or paragraphs, or the student participates in shorter lessons or parts of lessons.

Key considerations in reducing content are similar to our earlier question in that the IEP team must determine and focus on the most important knowledge within the broad curriculum goals specified for a given grade level. The role of state content and achievement standards in this process cannot be underestimated. The purpose of content standards is to define that critical set of knowledge. It is important to understand that teachers may include in their units of instruction and lesson plans instructional objectives and activities that go beyond the core standards. If the IEP team must limit the amount of content a student learns, the team must know the essential knowledge specified in the standards and not just pick skills from the curriculum that might be easiest to teach or easiest for the student to learn. In addition to state standards, examples we provided in Chapter 3 are helpful in making decisions about what to teach.

Box 6.4 shows an example of how goals and standards should be related.

The modified goals in the example in Box 6.4 are only 2 of perhaps as many as 10 or 12 that define the general education curriculum goals of one fourth-grade math standard related to spatial sense, measurement, and geometry. It is obvious from this example that the process of goal setting can become enormously complex and time consuming if teachers approach the IEP development as parallel activity that tries to restate standards or general education curriculum goals.

Instead, special education teachers need to be familiar with the underlying intended achievement that one would expect to see if the student is making progress toward proficiency in the essential areas of the curriculum. Once the IEP team clearly understands what they want to "see" the student do, the team has a better understanding of how to develop annual goals that reflect the desired student performance intended in the standard.

The IEP team will also need to consider whether the student needs instructional accommodations related to the curriculum modifications as well as other

Box 6.4 Relationship of Goals to Standards

Standard: The learner will demonstrate an understanding of, and be able to apply, the properties and relationships in geometry and standard units of measurement.

General Education Curricular Goal: Use manipulatives, pictorial representations, and appropriate vocabulary to identify properties of polyhedra; identify polyhedra in the environment.

Modified Goal: Use a variety of manipulatives, pictures, and real-life objects to demonstrate properties and shapes of familiar objects in the student's home and school environments.

General Education Curricular Goal: Estimate and measure length, capacity, and mass using these units: inches, yards, miles, centimeters, meters, kilometers; milliliters, cups, and pints; kilograms and tons.

Modified Goal: Estimate and measure length, area, and capacity of familiar objects and places in the student's home and school environments using inches, cups, and pints.

areas of the curriculum, and if so, which ones? Is there an accommodation that can augment existing skills and abilities? Can an accommodation compensate for, or bypass, the student's disability without altering the learning task itself?

What Specialized Interventions Will Be Required?

Not only will the IEP team need to determine how the modified curriculum IEP goals will be addressed, but they will also need to consider additional educational needs of the students in areas beyond the general curriculum. The team must address these in the IEP and specify annual goals.

Will We Set Alternate Achievement Standards?

Alternate achievement standards apply to a few students, typically those with significant cognitive disabilities, who may have highly individualized annual IEP goals and objectives or benchmarks. The annual goals are to be based within the same content areas reflected in the state standards but will reflect very different knowledge and skill requirements.

During the time a class is working on a unit on electricity and magnetism, a student who has goals based on alternate standards might complete a unit on personal safety with electricity. The student might use a different set of instructional materials than is used by the rest of the class. For example, a student with reading problems might use books or simple reading materials during a literature class or may only be able to use an assistive technology device to access and respond to information.

Annual IEP goals should clearly specify the expectations and outcomes in terms of what knowledge is to be gained and what the student is to do with that knowledge. IEP goals based on alternate achievement standards should be developed with the same long-term multiyear perspective. That is, the IEP team needs to be clear about why certain knowledge or skills have been selected and what impact these skills will have on long-term educational outcomes. The goals should also be measurable and attainable within the constraints of the instructional time and the instructional environments available to the student. Teachers should be less concerned about how elegantly the goals are stated and focus more on their accuracy as instructional targets. The elements of immediacy and specificity discussed in Chapter 2 should be considered here.

The IEP goals should also be aligned with the alternate assessments required by the state. Finally, IEP goals based on alternate achievement standards should reflect challenging expectations for the student. Goals should not be mired in low-level skills. However, at the same time, they should reflect the critical academic and functional skills essential to a student's future.

IEP OBJECTIVES AND BENCHMARKS

The 2004 IDEA amendments removed the requirement that IEPs have goals as well as objectives and benchmarks, except, as we noted earlier, for those students who will be held to alternate achievement standards. Changing the requirement to develop objectives is seen as reducing paperwork associated with the IEP and also intended to lead to IEPs that are more challenging and better aligned with state standards and the general education curriculum.

Yet, objectives and benchmarks can provide important information to parents, students, and teachers about the specifics of what is to be taught. Objectives are the smaller steps on the map to the ultimate performance targets specified by IEP goals. However, recall that in Chapter 2, we discussed the balance that must be struck between establishing highly observable and measurable objectives and larger, more general statements of curriculum goals. Use of benchmarks is one way to strike this balance.

If objectives define specific steps, benchmarks are the stops along the way to the IEP goals. Benchmarks are the exemplars of performance expected at key points during the school year. For general educators, these frequently translate into instructional units or blocks of instruction delivered during a grading period or semester. In the example in Box 6.4, the goals also would have critical benchmarks and indicators. For example, the student might be expected to use the linear measures to compute length, width, and distance of a variety of real objects at the beginning of the school year, but by the end of the first grading period, the student might be expected to use linear measures to solve word problems. These early benchmarks would be followed by others, addressing other measurement skills for the next period and so forth. If a teacher wanted more specificity, objectives could be written in conjunction with the benchmarks.

Again, thinking of a road map, if you are starting in New York and driving to Los Angeles, you would need to project where you will be each night. The route you take or the speed you choose to travel may be determined based on your own needs or plans, much as you set objectives. However, each day you must monitor your progress and adjust your plans if necessary. So, too, must the IEP provide the map from which teachers, parents, and students design their journey of learning. A word of caution is in order here. The traditional way of writing IEP objectives, with some reference to percentage of mastery, will not be useful for creating objectives pertaining to complex thinking and problem solving. For example, what would it mean to say that a student is able to "write a descriptive paragraph with 85% accuracy"? Instead, IEP teams must think about objectives as a way of locating a student on some continuum of performance. Over time, the student would be expected to move along the continuum in the direction of expertise.

MAKING THE LINK BETWEEN IEP GOALS AND STATE ASSESSMENTS

The link between IEP goals and state and district assessments is critical in this era of high-stakes accountability. The key idea to remember in setting IEP goals is that they should state clear performance targets based on grade-level achievement standards and curriculum that clearly define expected student performance across multiple years. Decisions about goals impact a student's opportunity to learn and also affect how prepared a student will be when the time comes for that student to be assessed.

If the assessments are used to make high-stakes decisions (such as promotion, retention, or graduation), then decisions about goals have serious implications for a student. IEP goals that do not clearly link to the general education curriculum might not address important subject matter that will be assessed. This may mean that a student does not receive a diploma or a school may be subject to consequences. IEP teams must think about the link between goals and assessment.

First, the assessment process used to develop IEP goals should generate multiple types of evidence of the student's level of performance. This body of evidence should consist primarily (if not entirely) of classroom- and curriculum-based measures rather than formal tests. Minimally, before writing a goal, the team will want to collect multiple samples of the student's work or performance in a variety of relevant and meaningful contexts. For example, before developing a written expression goal, various samples of writing on worksheets, journals, and letters might be collected pertaining to social studies, math, and language arts. The team also would want to obtain information pertaining to the student's use of the targeted knowledge or skill from the student's parents (e.g., observations and expectations regarding writing) and teachers (e.g., current and past teachers).

Second, the continuum of competence against which the student's performance will be judged should be included in the IEP. When a goal refers to a scoring rubric that is not part of a published assessment system (e.g., a state performance assessment program), that rubric should be attached directly to the IEP. When a scoring rubric associated with established state or district assessments is used, this rubric can simply be referenced. For example, an IEP goal in mathematics for a middle school student might look like this:

Expected Outcome

Willa will use variables in simple equations, inequalities, and formulas to solve two-step math problems.

Present Level of Performance

On five separate occasions, when presented with two-step math problems requiring use of variables, either developed by her teacher or sampled from the State Assessment Resource Kit, Willa's performance was scored by three different teachers at either "0" or "1" on the state's 5-point scoring rubric for mathematics problem solving.

Annual Goal

By May 12, 2006, Willa's performance in solving two-step math problems requiring use of variables will earn scores of "3" or "4" from at least three separate teachers using the state's 5-point scoring rubric for mathematics problem solving.

From IEP Goals to Instruction

The idea behind setting IEP goals that are referenced to state standards and the general education curriculum is that they will drive changes in where and how the student is instructed. However, this is neither easy nor automatic. Changing how we teach students is an important aspect of guaranteeing access to the general education curriculum. We already have discussed aspects of designing instruction that matches the demands of new standards-based curriculum. We also have addressed the important distinctions between accommodations and modifications. We have noted how IEP goals must be based on a comprehensive assessment of a student's current status in the general education curriculum.

Furthermore, before an IEP team modifies or changes the performance expectations for a student, the team must ensure that the overall conditions of instruction that exist in a classroom will enable the student to achieve the goals. Therefore, teachers need to examine current classroom practices and materials to determine the type and amount of accommodations needed by a particular student. Remember, just because a student may be entitled to accommodations, they should be considered only when the instruction in the general classrooms is unlikely to allow the student to access or progress in the curriculum. To the maximum extent possible, the instructional environment in the classroom should eliminate the need for accommodations and modifications. One way to accomplish this goal is through application of the principles of universal design for learning, discussed in Chapter 5.

It should be pretty obvious by now that special and general educators will be jointly responsible for providing students with disabilities access to the general education curriculum. This will require that teachers engage in a variety of collaborative activities, including joint planning, consultation, and co-teaching. In addition, special and general educators need to participate together in professional development designed to help them develop standards-based instruction. They should collaborate, with families, in school improvement planning and similar school-based activities related to raising the achievement of every student in a school. In other words, there must be collective responsibility for providing every student meaningful and effective access to the general education curriculum.

We know that general and special educator collaboration is a key feature of schools that work successfully for students with and without disabilities (Caron & McLaughlin, 2003). These schools are defined by a common set of characteristics including:

- A clearly defined core curriculum and set of performance standards that *every* teacher understands and can articulate. At the high school level, this is specific to subject matter areas, whereas at the elementary and middle school levels, faculty share an interest in the total curriculum.

- Clear annual school improvement targets, based on student data that include student performance on assessments; parent/community perceptions of the school; student attendance, suspensions, expulsions; and school climate.

- Expectations that every teacher contributes to achieving the school improvement goals and must be involved in the overall school improvement planning process. Often, teachers and parents work in small groups to focus on a particular improvement goal or to collect and examine data and develop strategies.

- Time and opportunity through a variety of venues to problem solve and share ideas and strategies—as a faculty, in small groups, and between individual teachers.

- A shared language among special and general education teachers that centers on curriculum goals and assessments. There is no talk of "your student" or "my student," but "our student."

- Clearly articulated expectations that *every* child in the school can achieve at higher levels and that achievement is valued among all students.

- Students are not "blamed" for low achievement, and no teacher abdicates responsibility for teaching the curriculum just because a student is in special education. *All* teachers accept responsibility for helping *all* students progress and achieve. In addition to these important characteristics, schools that focus on providing every student access to the general education curriculum engage in co-teaching, consultation, and collaboration.

Special and General Education Collaboration

There are different approaches to special and general education collaboration that are commonly used in classrooms. Most common are co-teaching and collaborative consultation (see Friend & Cook, 1996). Both approaches are characterized by equality between teachers or individuals in terms of responsibilities and roles. They also involve shared problem solving and planning. Examples of collaboration to provide access to the general curriculum are shown in Boxes 6.5 and 6.6.

Collaboration can take many forms, as the examples illustrate, but for most teachers in most situations, the need for a balance of authority and responsibility works best. Working collaboratively to assess educational progress and design interventions is best. Even better is having ongoing support and feedback as the strategy or intervention is implemented.

Co-Teaching

Co-teaching is an increasingly common instructional collaboration model that general and special education teachers use to help students access the general education curriculum. As the name implies, co-teaching means that at least one general and one special educator together provide instruction to a group of special and general education students in the same classroom. The principles of co-teaching are similar to team teaching, with the exception that the special educator's primary responsibility is to ensure that students with disabilities in the classroom are accessing the curriculum and otherwise working toward the goals of their IEPS. But, the co-teaching model offers opportunities to meet the needs of a diverse group of students.

Box 6.5 An Example of Collaboration: Watertown School District

Watertown school district has a long history of supporting special education students in general education classrooms. Very few students are educated outside of general education classrooms for any period of time. Special and general educators collaborate and team-teach, and paraeducators are available in the schools to assist general and special education teachers with special education students.

The district has strong expectations that students with disabilities will participate in the district curriculum and be held accountable for achieving state standards.

Despite the high level of support, both special and general education teachers are concerned about the level of the state standards and the number of concepts and skills they must teach. This has resulted in an accelerated pace of instruction and more and more students needing expanded opportunities for review and reinforcement of skills.

General and special educators have structured co-planning time and work collaboratively. They have had extensive joint professional development and have a great deal of professional discretion in how to best structure their interactions and instructional groups. General and special education teachers work very hard to ensure that students with disabilities have access to the curriculum. They share knowledge of the standards and the general curriculum and engage in discussions about how individual students are performing in the standards and curriculum. They do not focus on day-to-day lesson plans as much as they plan around units or larger segments of instruction that address specific standards. They load up on planning at the beginning of grading periods and before major instructional units, asking the following questions:

- Which standards will be addressed?
- What will students be expected to know and do at the end of the unit?
- Where are students with IEPs currently performing?
- What are the core and essential standards that every student should attain and which are relevant to student with IEPs?

The answers to these questions help determine the aspects of the curriculum that will be the focus of special education interventions provided by either the general or the special education teacher, or both. All teachers, as well as speech and language therapists and other specialists, have a clear idea of the outcomes a student is expected to achieve after instruction in the intended curriculum.

Box 6.6 Providing Access Through Collaboration

In a fifth-grade classroom, the teacher is presenting a lesson on Egypt and the pyramids. In this class of 23 students are 4 students with IEPs. Among the four students, one is functionally a nonreader, and the other three are about 2 to 3 years below grade level. All have poor attention, memory, and organization. One student has significant behavior difficulties and is on and off medication. Each child is seen separately by the special education teacher about 3 or 4 times a week for intensive instruction in reading and learning strategies.

Each student has a worksheet of a passage to read, followed by questions to be answered. The questions have been modified for the students with IEPs. The lesson addresses several of the state standards in history and reading. The teacher leads a lively discussion with the entire class, using guided questioning to explain why pyramids were built and how they related to religious aspects of Egyptian culture. Then, students break into four discussion groups to read the passage and answer the questions as a group. The students with IEPs participate in the whole class instruction, but during independent seatwork, a general education teacher, an aide, and peers support the individual students. Groups are then re-formed for direct skill instruction. The students with IEPs and one other student requiring remediation meet as a group with the special education teacher who does a lesson on pyramids, asking, "Who, What, When, and Where" questions. There is lively discussion about the most important aspects of building the pyramids. Students take turns dictating sentences (using "who," "what," "when," and "where") and critiquing one another's sentences.

What's right with this example?

- The teachers share a common vision of the key concepts and knowledge to be addressed in the lesson.
- There is active sharing of responsibility for instruction.

What needs improvement in this example?

- Perhaps students with disabilities should not be taken out of the discussion, as they could profit from the language and ideas that are being expressed. These ideas could later be expanded or paraphrased through guided question and answer in a small group.

Friend and Cook (1996) describe five co-teaching approaches:

1. One teaching, one supporting
2. Station teaching
3. Parallel teaching

4. Alternative teaching
5. Team teaching

One teaching/one supporting is the most common form of co-teaching and the easiest to implement. In this model, one teacher has the primary role of designing and delivering instruction while the second teacher floats, helping and observing individual students. A major downside to this model is that too often it is based on having all children learn the same content in the same manner. This means that the special educator's role is to help students keep up or catch up rather than to design individualized accommodations or differentiate instruction. In some classrooms, the special educator functions almost like an instructional assistant in the classroom. In other classrooms, the general and special educators take turns leading a lesson. Aside from the inequities in roles that this approach to co-teaching may create, it does not result in genuine access to the general curriculum for the students.

When two teachers station-teach, they divide the content or lesson, and each is individually responsible for planning and teaching part of it to some part of the class. Students move through both teacher-led groups. Each teacher teaches every student but in small groups. In this model, the special educator functions like another teacher in terms of responsibility for the curriculum.

Parallel teaching involves joint planning, and each teacher delivers the same content and instruction to half the class. This type of co-teaching is best for drill exercises or when the content is so specific that the instruction in both groups is similar.

Alternative teaching is probably the second most common form of special and general education co-teaching. In this model, special and general educators jointly plan instruction, but the special educator focuses on re-teaching or reinforcing materials taught, differentiating instruction, and making curricular accommodations and modifications for small groups of students that may need extra assistance. This model can work for any student who may need some additional help. It is important in implementing this model not to stigmatize or otherwise dumb down the curriculum content. Furthermore, special and general education teachers must be clear about the core and essential knowledge that the students are expected to learn.

Finally, team teaching requires equal planning and equal roles in implementing instruction. In fact, in a team-teaching arrangement, individual teams may use all or any of the strategies discussed above. Teachers will trade off roles and groups of students.

Any or all of the above strategies will only be effective if the collaborating teachers have equal status in the classroom and recognize what knowledge and skills each brings to the collaborative effort.

CONCLUSION

In this chapter, we have presented a model framework for developing individual student IEPs that are truly aligned with state content and achievement standards and the general education curriculum. This is not an easy process, nor can it be done quickly or without a sound understanding of the meaning of curriculum, purposes of assessment, and how to match curriculum demands to instruction—all topics that we have addressed in this book. What is more, we have clearly indicated that in today's climate of high-stakes accountability, providing students with disabilities access to the general education curriculum is even more important to schools and to individual students.

When we completed the first edition of this book, the 1997 IDEA amendments were just becoming reality in the schools and the meaning of "access to the general curriculum" was unclear to many; in addition, the No Child Left Behind Act (NCLB) had not yet been passed by Congress. Now as we complete this second edition, we find a New IDEA with even stronger language linking special education to general education, specifically to requirements that all students with disabilities access one set of state content standards and participate in state assessments and accountability. In today's schools, the New IDEA and NCLB are intertwined, and all teachers and practitioners must focus on improving the performance levels of all students. With this new emphasis on results, every teacher needs to fully understand what it means to provide access to the general education curriculum in a way that leads to increasing levels of achievement and ultimately better school outcomes.

Appendix A

Resources For Facilitating Access

National Association of State Directors of Special Education (NASDSE)

The NASDSE promotes and supports education programs for students with disabilities in the United States and outlying areas. NASDSE is a not-for-profit corporation established in 1938 and operates for the purpose of providing services to state agencies to facilitate their efforts to maximize educational outcomes for individuals with disabilities.

NASDSE
1800 Diagonal Road, Suite 320
Alexandria, VA 22314
Phone: (703) 519-3800; Fax: (703) 519-3808; TDD: (703) 519-7008
Web site: http://www.nasdse.org/home.htm

National Center on Educational Outcomes (NCEO)

The NCEO provides national leadership in the participation of students with disabilities and limited English proficient (LEP) students in national and state assessments, standards-setting efforts, and graduation requirements.

National Center on Educational Outcomes
University of Minnesota
350 Elliott Hall, 75 East River Road
Minneapolis, MN 55455
Phone: (612) 626-1530; Fax: (612) 624-0879
Web site: http://education.umn.edu/NCEO/

Learn About Your Own State Standards

Visit your state department of education Web site. You'll find important information regarding your state's content and achievement standards, assessments, accommodation policies, and curricula. To find the Web site for your state, use a search engine such as Google or Yahoo. Type in

(*your state's name*) Department of Education
Here are some examples:
Nebraska Department of Education
Result: http://www.nde.state.ne.us/
Indiana Department of Education
Result: http://ideanet.doe.state.in.us/
New Mexico Department of Education
Result: http://www.ped.state.nm.us/div/fin/trans/
Missouri Department of Education
Result: http://www.dese.state.mo.us/

Resources for the 2004 Reauthorization of the Individuals with Disabilities Education Act (IDEA)

Council for Exceptional Children (CEC) is the largest international professional organization dedicated to improving educational outcomes for individuals with exceptionalities, students with disabilities, and the gifted. CEC advocates for appropriate governmental policies, sets professional standards, provides continual professional development, advocates for newly and historically underserved individuals with exceptionalities, and helps professionals obtain conditions and resources necessary for effective professional practice.

The Council for Exceptional Children
1920 Association Drive
Reston, VA 20191–1589
Toll-free: 1-888-CEC-SPED; Local: (703) 620-3660
TTY (text only): (703) 264-9446; Fax: (703) 264-9494
Web site: http://www.cec.sped.org

The CEC maintains an online catalog of information pertaining to the topic of accessing the general education curriculum. You can access this catalog at

http://www.cec.sped.org/bk/catalog2/access.html

Wrightslaw

Wrightslaw provides information about special education law and advocacy for children with disabilities. The Web site is maintained by Peter W. D. Wright, an attorney specializing in special education law, and Pamela Darr Wright, a psychotherapist and editor of the *Special Education Advocate*. The site includes articles, cases, newsletters, and resources about a wide variety of topics. A downloadable version of *The Special Education Advocate* also is available on the Web site. The address for the Wrightslaw Web site is

http://www.wrightslaw.com/law/idea/index.htm

Resources for No Child Left Behind

No Child Left Behind: A Tool Kit for Teachers

This U.S. Department of Education document provides extensive information and resources for schools working to implement No Child Left Behind. The tool kit was updated in 2004 and will be periodically updated again as new policies and legislation develop. You can download the tool kit from

http://www.ed.gov/teachers/nclbguide/nclb-teachers-toolkit.pdf

What Works Clearinghouse

The What Works Clearinghouse (WWC) collects, screens, and identifies studies of the effectiveness of educational programs, products, practices, and policies. The Clearinghouse reviews the studies that have the strongest design and reports on the strengths and weaknesses of those studies against the WWC Evidence Standards, which are based on the U.S. Department of Education's definition of scientifically based research. The WWC can be accessed at

http://www.whatworks.ed.gov/

Professional Development Resources About Accessing the General Curriculum

The IRIS Center for Faculty Development

The IRIS Center for Faculty Enhancement is funded by the U.S. Department of Education's Office of Special Education Programs and primarily serves college faculty working in pre-service preparation programs. The center aims to ensure that general education teachers, school administrators, school nurses, and school counselors are well prepared to work with students who have disabilities and with their families. IRIS is the nation's only faculty enhancement center established for this purpose. The IRIS Center has a wide variety of professional development resources available online. You can access a module that specifically addresses access to the general education curriculum at the IRIS Center Web site:

http://iris.peabody.vanderbilt.edu/HST/cresource.htm

The Regional Education Laboratory Network

The Regional Educational Laboratories are educational research and development organizations supported by contracts with the U.S. Education Department, Institute of Education Sciences (IES; formerly known as the Office of Educational Research and Improvement [OERI]). The network provides a vast amount of material on curricula, instruction, and professional development. These resources are appropriate for the majority of children with high incidence disabilities. Follow the link to the lab in your region by the context-sensitive map at

http://www.nwrel.org/national/

Center for Effective Collaboration and Practice

The U.S. Department of Education's Office of Special Education Programs has funded a center to work with other federal agencies to surmount the barriers to collaboration and knowledge use in the multidisciplinary, multistakeholder, multiethnic context in which children with emotional and behavioral problems live and are served. The Center for Effective Collaboration and Practice is engaging in a series of strategic activities designed to help special education communities develop a greater capacity to produce, access, and use information, and to collaborate.

Center for Effective Collaboration and Practice
American Institutes for Research
1000 Thomas Jefferson St. NW, Suite 400
Washington, DC 20007
Toll Free: (888) 457-1551; Local: (202) 944-5400
Web site: http://www.air.org/ehd/ehd_special_ed.aspx
E-mail: center@air-dc.org

Resources for Universal Design

The Center for Applied Special Technology (CAST)

CAST is a not-for-profit organization whose mission is to expand opportunities for individuals with disabilities through the development and innovative use of technology. Cast is accessible at

http://www.cast.org
Resources available through CAST include:
Universal Design for Access and for Learning at
http://www.cast.org/udl/UDforAccessLearning9.cfm
Teaching strategies, including adapting curricula at
http://www.cast.org/udl/CoreConcepts6.cfm
Teaching tools at
http://www.cast.org/tools

National Center on Accessing the General Curriculum

The National Center on Accessing the General Curriculum (NCAC) provides a vision of how new curricula, teaching practices, and policies can be woven together to create practical approaches for improved access to the general curriculum by students with disabilities. The NCAC was established by CAST in a collaborative agreement with the U.S. Department of Education's Office of Special Programs (OSEP). NCAC extends the work of CAST by providing professional development and innovative evidence-based educational products. The Web site for NCAC is

http://www.cast.org/ncac/AboutNCAC371.cfm

Center for Universal Design

This center is a national research, information, and technical assistance center that evaluates, develops, and promotes universal design in housing, public and commercial facilities, and related products. The Center for Universal Design is housed at North Carolina State University and can be accessed at

http://www.design.ncsu.edu/cud/index.html

Trace Research and Development Center

Trace is a research center at the University of Wisconsin–Madison, which focuses on making off-the-shelf technologies and systems (e.g., computers, the Internet, and information kiosks) more accessible for everyone through the process known as universal, or accessible, design. The Trace Web site is

http://www.trace.wisc.edu/

Resources for Learning and Technology

Bransford, J. D., Brown, A. L., Cocking, R. R., & Pellegrino, J. W. (Eds.). (2000). *How people learn: Bridging research and practice.* Washington, DC: National Academy Press.

This book provides an overview of the most recent research on human learning, with specific reference to implications for classroom practice. The book also presents a research agenda for strengthening THE link between what we know about learning and what goes on in U.S. schools. An electronic version of the book can be accessed at

http://www.nap.edu/html/howpeople1/

The Learning Technology Center (LTC)

The LTC is a research center at Vanderbilt University´s Peabody College of Education. The LTC is a group of 70 researchers, designers, and educators who are internationally known for their work on technology in education. Members´ skills and knowledge cover a wide range of areas including Education, Psychology, Computer Science, Mathematics, Chemistry, Organizational Administration, Public Policy, and Video and Multimedia Design. The Web site for the LTC is

http://www.cilt.org/

The LTC also supports the **K–12 Learning Consortium**: a technology-supported project for exploring, disseminating, and sustaining new visions of student learning. The mission of the Learning Consortium is to improve education through collaboration enhanced by technology. The Consortium is working to help a variety of education stakeholders appreciate the importance of learning with understanding (vs. memorizing facts and procedures) and to do so, in part, by focusing attention on classroom-based activities enhanced by the use of frequent assessments for guiding and monitoring learning. Reach these resources at

http://canvas.ltc.vanderbilt.edu/lc

References

Armstrong, D. G. (1989). *Developing and documenting the curriculum.* Needham Heights, MA: Allyn & Bacon.

Barnett, D., Daly, E., Jones, K., & Lenz, E. (2004). Response to intervention: Empirically based special service decision from single case designs of increasing and decreasing intensity. *The Journal of Special Education, 38*(2), 66–79.

Berliner, D. C. (1990). What's all the fuss about instructional time? In M. Ben-Pertz & R. Bromme (Eds.), *The nature of time in schools: Theoretical concepts, practitioner perceptions.* New York: Teachers College Press.

Bloom, B. S., Engelhart, M. D., Furst, E. J., Hill, W. H., & Krathwohl, D. R. (1956). *Taxonomy of educational objectives: Cognitive domain.* New York: Longman.

Bransford, J. D., Brown, A. L., & Cocking, R. R. (Eds.). (2000). *How people learn: Brain, mind, experience, and school* (Expanded ed.). Washington, DC: National Academy of Sciences.

Browder, D. M., Spooner, F., Ahlgrim-Delzell, L., Flowers, C., Karvonen, M., & Algozzine, B. (in press). A content analysis of the curricular philosophies reflected in states' alternate assessments. *Research and Practice for Persons with Severe Disabilities.*

Caron, E. A., & McLaughlin, M. J. (2003). Indicators of "Beacons of Excellence" schools: Collaborative practices. *Journal of Educational and Psychological Consultation, 13*(4), 285–313.

Case, R. (1985). *Intellectual development: Birth to Adulthood.* San Diego, CA: Academic Press.

Cuban, L. (1993). The lure of curricular reform and its pitiful history. *Phi Delta Kappan, 75*(2), 181–185.

CTB McGraw-Hill. (2000). *Terra Nova* (2nd ed.). California Achievement Test–6. Monterey, CA: Author.

Deno, S. L. (1985). Curriculum-based measurement: The emerging alternative. *Exceptional Children, 52*, 219–232.

Espin, C. A., Scierka, B. J., Skare, S., & Halverson, N. (1999). Criterion-related validity of curriculum-based measures in writing for secondary students. *Reading and Writing Quarterly, 15*, 5–27.

Freeman, D. J., & Porter, A. C. (1989). Do textbooks dictate the content of mathematics instruction in elementary schools? *American Educational Research Journal, 26*(3), 403–421.

Friend, M., & Cook, L. (1996). *Interactions: Collaboration skills for school professionals.* New York: Longman.

Fuchs, D., Mock, D., Morgan, P., & Young, C. (2003). Responsiveness-to-intervention: Definitions, evidence, and implications for the learning disabilities construct. *Learning Disabilities Research & Practice, 18*(3), 157–171.

Fuchs, L. S. (1998). Computer applications to address implementation difficulties associated with curriculum-based measurement. In M. Shinn (Ed.), *Advanced applications of curriculum-based measurement* (pp. 89–112). New York: Guilford Press.

Gagne, R. M. (1974). *Essentials of learning for instruction.* New York: Dryden Press.

Gagne, R. M. (1988). Mastery learning and instructional design. *Performance Improvement Quarterly, 1*(1), 7–18.

Gerber, M. M. (2003, December). *Teachers are still the test: Limitations of response to instruction strategies for identifying children with learning disabilities.* Paper presented at the National Research Center on Learning Disabilities Responsiveness-to-Intervention Symposium, Kansas City, MO.

Harper, R. A. (1990). Geography's role in general education. *Journal of Geography, 89*(5), 214–218.

Hoover, H. D., Hieronymus, A. N., Frisbie, D. A., & Dunbar, S. A (1993). *Iowa Test of Basic Skills.* Chicago: Riverside.

Howell, K., & Nolet, V. W. (2000). *Curriculum-based evaluation* (3rd ed.). Atlanta, GA: Wadsworth.

Hudson, P., Lignugaris-Kraft, & Miller, M. (1993). Using content enhancements to improve the performance of adolescents with learning disabilities in content classes. *Learning Disabilities Research & Practice, 8*(2), 106–126.

Laurent-Brennan, C. (1998). The International Baccalaureate Program. *Clearing House, 71*(4), 197–198.

Lenz, K., Bulgren, J. A., & Hudson, P. (1990). Content enhancement: A model for promoting acquisition of content by individuals with learning disabilities. In T. E. Scruggs & B. L. Y. Wong (Eds.), *Intervention and research in learning disabilities* (pp. 122–165). New York: Springer-Verlag.

Lewis, R. (1993). *Special education technology: Classroom applications.* Atlanta, GA: Wadsworth.

Mager, R. F. (1997). *Preparing instructional objectives: A critical tool in the development of effective instruction.* Atlanta, GA: Center for Effective Performance.

Marsh, C., & Willis, G. (1995). *Curriculum: Alternative approaches, ongoing issues.* Englewood Cliffs, NJ: Merrill/Prentice Hall.

McLaughlin, M. J., Henderson, K., & Rhim, L. M. (1997). *Snapshots of reform: A report of reform in five local school districts.* Alexandria, VA: Center for Policy Research on the Impact of General and Special Education Reform, National Association of State Boards of Education.

McLaughlin, M. J., Nagle, K. M., Nusz, C., Ruedel, K., Lazarus, S., Thompson, S., et al. (in press). *Inclusion of students with disabilities in assessments and accountability reforms in four states: Considerations for analysis of the achievement gap* (Topical Review No. 7). College Park: University of Maryland, Institute for the Study of Exceptional Children and Youth, Educational Policy Reform Research Institute.

McLaughlin, M. J., Nolet, V., Rhim, L. M., & Henderson, K. (1999). Integrating standards: Including all students. *Teaching Exceptional Children, 31*(3), 66–71.

Nagle, K. M. (2004). *Emerging state-level themes: Strengths and stressors in educational accountability reform* (Topical Review No. 4). College Park: University of Maryland, Educational Policy Reform Research Institute. Available from www.eprri.org

Orkwis, R., & McLane, K. (1998). *A curriculum every student can use: Design principles for student access* (ERIC/OSEP Topical Brief). Reston, VA: ERIC Clearinghouse on Disabilities and Gifted Education, Council for Exceptional Children.

Posner, G. J., & Strike, K. A. (1976). A categorization scheme for principles of sequencing content. *Review of Educational Research, 46*(4), 665–690.

Pugach, M. C., & Warger, C. L. (1993). Curriculum considerations. In J. I. Goodlad & T. C. Lovitt (Eds.), *Integrating general and special education* (pp. 125–148). New York: Merrill-Macmillan.

Rose, D. H., & Meyer, A. (2002). Teaching *every student in the digital age: Universal design for learning.* Alexandria, VA: Association for Supervision and Curriculum Development.

Shriner, J. G., & DeStefano, L. (2003). Participation and accommodation in state assessment: The role of Individualized Education Programs. *Exceptional Children, 26*(2), 9–16.

Smith, P. L., & Ragan, T. J. (2005). *Instructional Design* (3rd ed). Hoboken, NJ: Wiley.

Stodolsky, S. S. (1988). *The subject matters: Classroom activity in math and social studies.* Chicago: University of Chicago Press.

Tindal, G. R., & Marston, D. (1990). *Classroom-based assessment: Evaluating instructional outcomes.* Columbus, OH: Merrill.

Williams, R. G., & Haladyna, T. M. (1982). Logical operations for generating intended questions (LOGIQ): A typology for higher order level test items. In G. H. Roid & T. M. Haladyna (Eds.), *A technology for test-item writing* (pp. 161–186). New York: Academic Press.

Wineburg, S. S. (1991). On the reading of historical texts: Notes on the breach between school and academy. *American Educational Research Journal, 28*(3), 495–519.

Index

The Corwin Press logo—a raven striding across an open book—represents the union of courage and learning. Corwin Press is committed to improving education for all learners by publishing books and other professional development resources for those serving the field of K–12 education. By providing practical, hands-on materials, Corwin Press continues to carry out the promise of its motto: **"Helping Educators Do Their Work Better."**